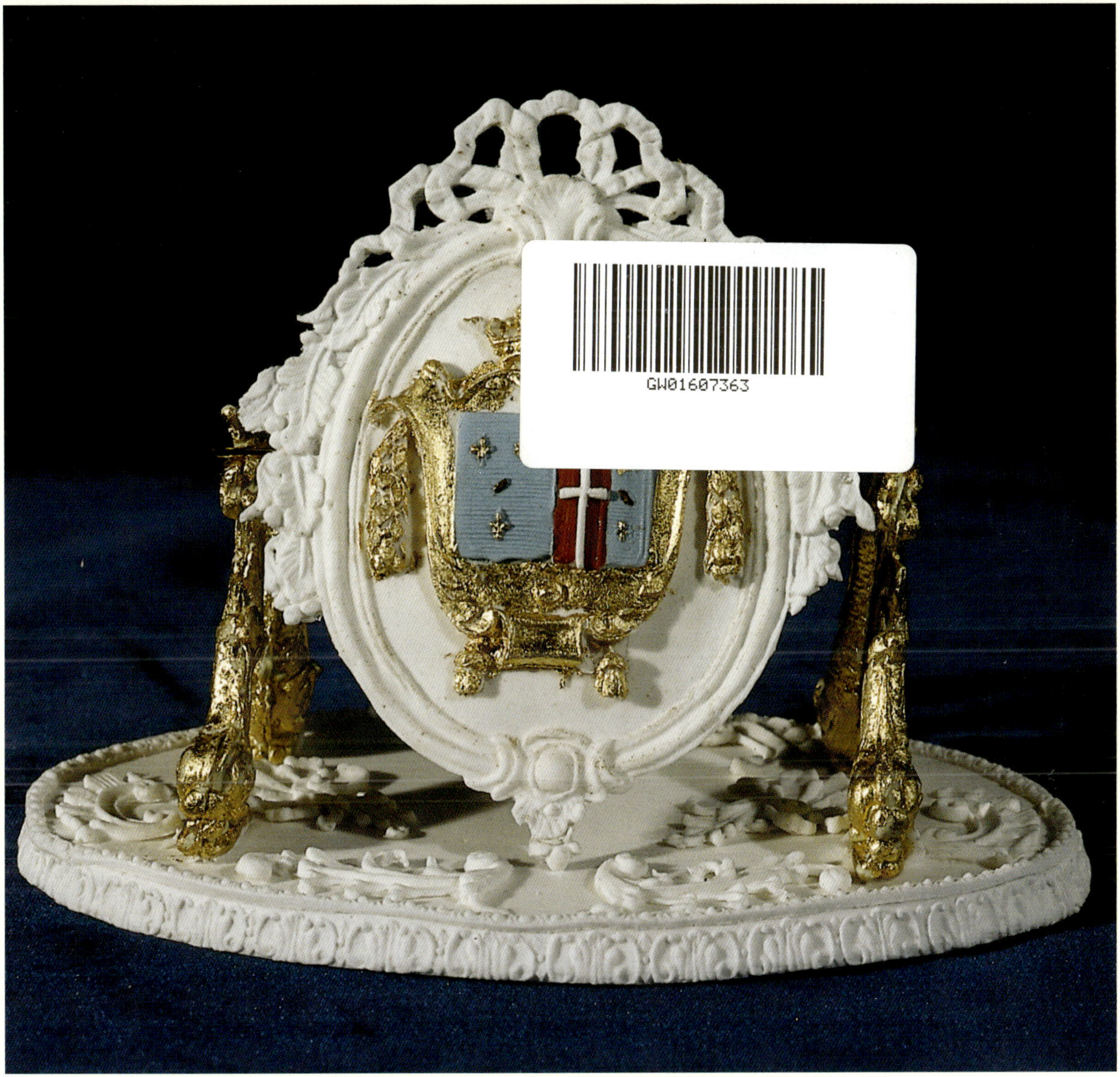

Plate 1 (see page 37) Sugar-paste cartouche on a stand made up from gilded sugar dolphins. The arms are those of the Princesse de Lamballe, Marie-Thérèse Louise de Savoie-Carignan (1749-92), who was a favourite and close friend of Marie-Antoinette. Made from a French hardwood confectioner's mould of the late 1780s.

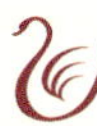

Foreword

The Bowes Museum is proud to present the remarkable exhibition *Royal Sugar Sculpture: 600 Years of Splendour* in 2002, to mark Her Majesty Queen Elizabeth's Golden Jubilee. The idea for this exhibition arose from the fruitful collaboration between our Keeper of Ceramics, Dr. Howard Coutts, and international food historian Ivan Day in 1994 in the exhibition *The Tempting Table: European Table Layout 1500-1870*, based on The Bowes Museum's extensive holdings of European ceramics of the period 1500-1900. Their research has culminated in the acquisition this year, with support from the National Art Collections Fund and the Heritage Lottery Fund, of a remarkable collection of French 19th century moulds for sugar-paste decoration, together with associated drawings demonstrating how the pieces were set up.

The creation of sugar sculpture was almost invariably associated with feasts of royal status, and so we have chosen this Royal Golden Jubilee year to invite Ivan Day, and his associates Peter Brears and Tony Barton, to recreate some of the remarkable pieces that are known to have graced royal tables in the past, and which otherwise survive only in description and illustration. This catalogue, which accompanies the exhibition, explores the history of this remarkable medium over the last 600 years.

Adrian Jenkins
Director

Acknowledgements

The Bowes Museum's collection of sugar moulds, tools and watercolours was bought with the aid of grants from the National Art Collections Fund and the Heritage Lottery Fund. We should like to thank Mary Yule, Suzanne Baker, Francesco Radaeli, and Jill Norman for their assistance in this matter.

This exhibition would not have been possible without the remarkable skills and knowledge of Peter Brears and Tony Barton. Others we would like to thank for their advice and assistance are:
Anne Allen, Bill Brown, Peter Brown, Maureen Cassidy-Geiger, Beverley Dutton, Laura Mason, David Mitchell, Ken Noble, Paul Rea, Vivien Reid, Gillian Riley, Lord Rothschild, Selma Schwartz, Lindsay Tuck, Charles Truman, Robin Weir, John Whitehead, Gill Whitehead.

The following individuals and organisations have kindly loaned items to this exhibition:

Peter Brears;

Robin Weir;

The Museum of London;

The National Trust, Waddesdon Manor, Buckinghamshire;

Wittelsbacher Ausgleichsfonds, courtesy of the Bayersiche Verwaltung der staatlichen Schlösser, Gärten und Seen, Munich;

Kunstgewerbemuseum, staatliche Kunstsammlungen, Dresden;

Scottish National Portrait Gallery, Edinburgh;

The Victoria and Albert Museum, London;

Norfolk Museums and Archaeology Service, Norwich;

Torquay Museum;

Birmingham Museums and Art Gallery;

The Brotherton Library, University of Leeds.

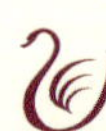

Contents

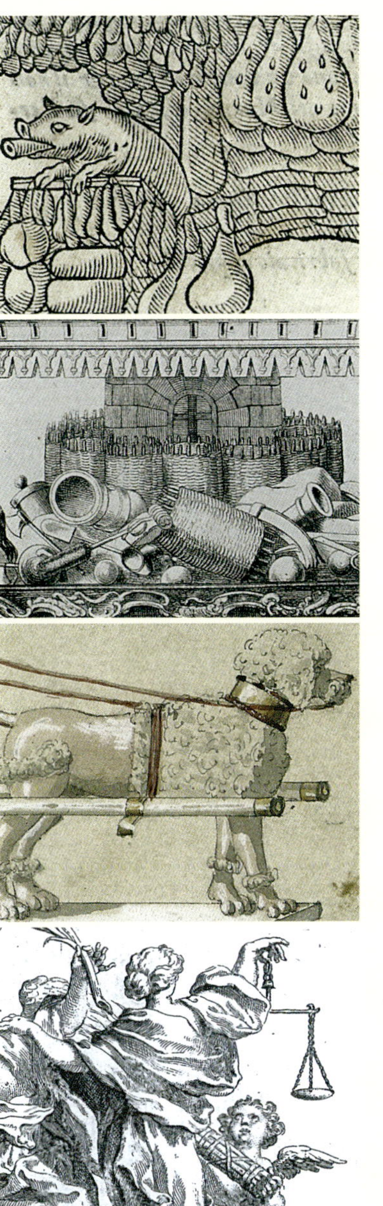

Introduction

Recently The Bowes Museum bought an important collection of early 19th century confectioner's moulds and designs of table ornaments. This acquisition has been the main reason behind developing the exhibition, which takes an in-depth, but by no means comprehensive, look at the history of European sugar art. The evolution of this curious style of sculpture is traced from a royal art form in the late medieval period to the popular revival of the craft in modern times.

Examples of this ephemeral art perished long ago, but a number of accounts, drawings, prints and moulds still survive to tell the tale. The exhibition brings together this scattered evidence for the first time.

The main focus of the exhibition is an authentic recreation of an early nineteenth century French dessert table setting, which has been made possible through the unique Bowes collection, most of which is also on display in the exhibition. Drawing on other rarely seen material, we have also been able to create accurate reconstructions of sugar sculptures taken from a number of actual historical feasts and festivals.

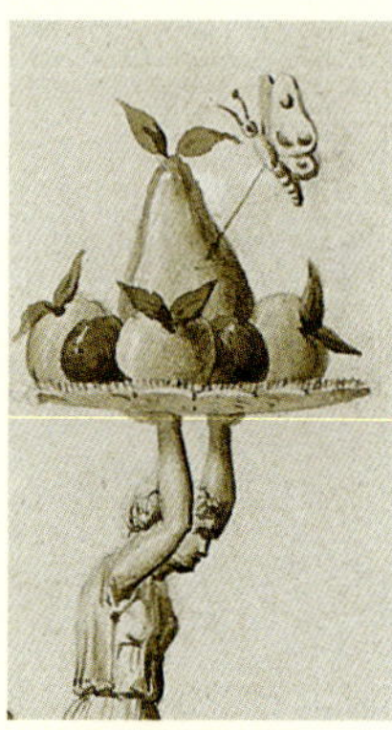

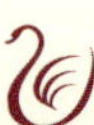

A Royal Art Form

Lavish table displays have always been a vital ingredient of royal entertainments and feasts. Buffets piled high to the ceiling with the finest silver, and tables spread with luxury foods, not only created a great sense of occasion, but also demonstrated the power and status of the monarchy. For events of state, coronations and bridal feasts, royal cooks and confectioners were frequently required to embellish their sovereign's table with impressive sculptural centrepieces fashioned from food materials, such as sugar and marzipan. From time to time, professional artists, rather than humble kitchen staff, were commissioned to produce work in this unusual genre. The great Renaissance sculptor, Jacopo Sansovino, designed sugar sculptures for Henry III of France when the King passed through Venice in 1574 on the way to his coronation. In 1655, the Pope honoured Queen Christina of Sweden with a table embellished with gilded sugar figures made by Johann Paul Schorr and Ercole Ferrata, two major baroque sculptors who collaborated with Gianlorenzo Bernini.

Art historians would probably hesitate before seriously considering these culinary extravaganzas as works of art, but the evidence from contemporary descriptions and drawings indicates that they were often made with the same consummate skill as sculpture in more orthodox materials. Just like more serious works, these transient creations frequently fulfilled a symbolic or allegorical role. At the wedding feast of Maria de' Medici to Henri IV in Florence in 1600, the groom chose to be absent, but his image appeared on the table in the form of an impressive equestrian statue, modelled in sugar by Pietro Tacca. In February 1815, a feast was given in the Great Hall of the Louvre by the Royal Guard to celebrate the final defeat of Napoleon and the return of the French monarchy. Huge *pièces montées*, in the form of gilded sugar military trophies, crafted by the patissier Carême, were displayed between the tables. Whether at a royal wedding or a victory banquet, food sculpture of this kind was frequently the artistic medium of choice.

Elaborate table decorations have now been unfashionable for the best part of a century. After the First World War, the triumph of modernism brought about an almost total rejection of ornament, while the growth of socialism and republican political systems led to a view that grand table displays of this kind were one of the worst forms of aristocratic excess. With a strong emphasis on utility and simplicity of design, the twentieth century table tended to be laid with a minimum of fuss. Even the surviving European royal households toned down the opulence of state meals to avoid accusations of extravagance. In an egalitarian age, floral centrepieces and displays of ancestral plate were acceptable, but six-foot high sugar sculptures of the sovereign's virtues were definitely not.

For most of the twentieth century the classical style of ornament, favoured by culinary artists since the Renaissance, found its sole refuge on the iced multi-tiered wedding cake. However, since the 1960s, 'hobby' cake decorators and sugar crafters in Britain have spearheaded a revival of many of the techniques, tools and materials of sugar sculpture. With the current growing interest in ephemeral art forms and the social history of food, it is timely that this whole phenomenon should be examined seriously.

Gum Paste and Cast Sugar

The methods and materials of sugar sculpture

Since antiquity, apothecaries have used the gum harvested from various species of Goat's Thorn or Tragacanth shrub (*Astragalus* spp.) as a binding material for making pills and other medicines from powdered drugs. Raw tragacanth is a ribbon-like exudate that forms on bark wounds on this thorny bush, which grows on arid mountain slopes all over the Eastern Mediterranean (plate 2). When steeped in water, gum tragacanth or gum dragon, (as it was once known in England), forms a sticky mucilage which allows any powdered material to be converted into a pliable, plasticine-like paste. Middle Eastern or Byzantine physicians and confectioners were probably the first to discover that when mixed with powdered sugar, tragacanth produces a fine edible modelling material of great flexibility. This material has been variously called sugar plate, pastillage, sugar paste and gum-paste. When dry, it is a beautiful white material with tremendous ornamental possibilities. It can be rolled out wafer-thin and fashioned into delicate petals for artificial flowers, or pressed into carved wooden moulds to create impressive animals or moulded features for sugar buildings. The paste can be coloured readily with dyes and pigments and, when dry, lends itself to painting or gilding.

The earliest printed recipe for gum-paste appeared in a book of secrets compiled by Girolamo Ruscelli, first published in Venice in 1552. Within a few years, Ruscelli's work had been translated into German, French and English, though the technique he describes seems to have been known to European court confectioners well before this time. The following recipe is from the London edition of 1558:

'To make a paste of sugre, wherof a man maye make all maner of fruites, and other fyne thynges, with theyr forme, as platters, dishes, glasses, cuppes, and such like thinges, wherwith you may furnish a table: and when you have doen, eate them up. A pleasant thing for them that sit at the table.

Take gomme dragant, as much as you will, and stiepe it in Rose water, until it be molified. And for foure onces of Sugre, take of it the bignes of a Beane, the iuyce of Lemons a walnut shell full, and a litle of the white of an egge: but you must first take the gomme, and beate it so much with a pestel in a morter of white marble, or of brasse until it become like water, then put to it the iuyce with the white of the egge, incorporating wel altogether. This dooen, take iii. onces of fine white sugre, well beaten to poulder, and cast it into the morter by litle and litle, untill all bee turned into the forme of paste. Then take it oute of the saied morter, and bray it upon the poulder of sugre, as it were meale or flowre, untill all bee like soft paste, to the ende you may turne it and facion it which way you wil. Whan you have brought your paste to this forme, spreade it abroade with Sinamon, upon greate or small leaves, as you shall thinke it good: and so shall you forme and make what things you wil, as is aforesated. this paste is verie delicate and savourous.'

An alternative way of making figures and ornamental sugar objects was to pour concentrated sugar syrup into wooden, ceramic or plaster moulds, and allow it to solidify into a candy. This technique, known as cast sugar, may be older than gum paste and also seems to have originated in the Middle East or Byzantium. However, the result is not as fine as that obtained with gum paste, as the surface of cast sugar has a grainy surface that is more difficult to decorate. Nevertheless, it allowed much larger and more robust sculpture to be produced. At an Ottoman festival in Istanbul in 1582, specialised artists known as *sukker nakkasarli* created several hundred cast sugar figures for a spectacular procession to commemorate the circumcision of the son of Sultan Murad III. These included giraffes, elephants, lions, fountains and castles, some of which were so large that they had to be carried by four people. This tradition seems to have been very well established in the city and may well predate the Ottoman invasion of 1453, as the *sukker nakkasarli* were from the ancient Byzantine Jewish community. The cast-sugar technique is still utilised in Mexico to create little sugar skulls, which are used to celebrate the

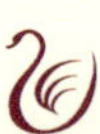

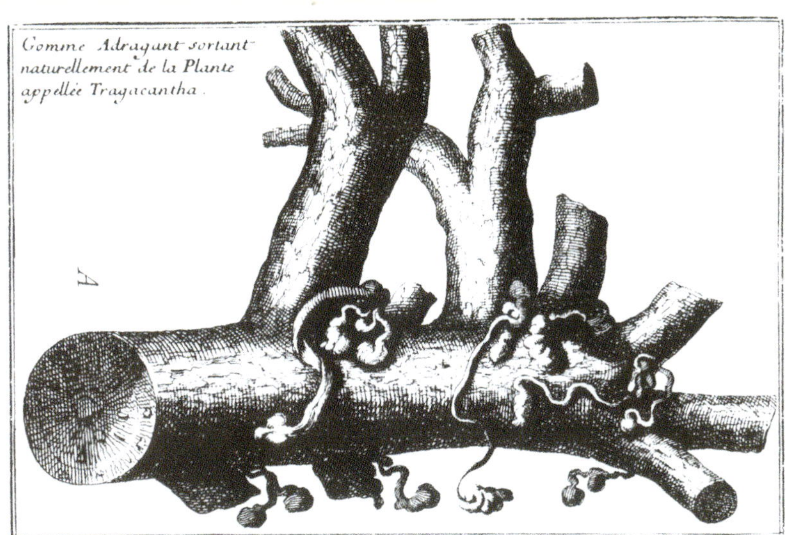

Plate 2 (see page 7)
Tragacanth. Illustration from Joseph Pitton de Tournefort, *Relation d'un Voyage du Levant*, Paris,1717. (Private Collection).

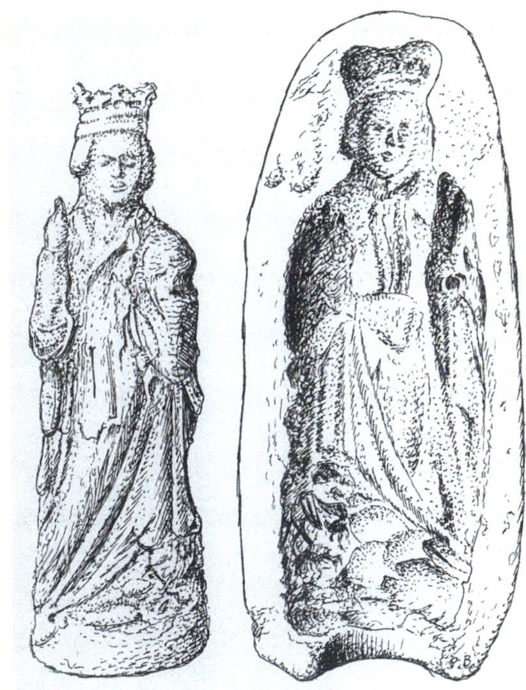

Plate 3 (see page 9)
A terracotta sugar mould of St. Catherine of Siena.
Late 15th/ early 16th century.
Museum of London. Line drawing by Peter Brears.

Day of the Dead. Remarkably, these are called *alfeniques* (from the Arabic *al fänäd* - candy), testifying to the Arab origin of the technique.

Sugar syrup cast in moulds also seems to have been a popular method for creating table ornaments in England and probably pre-dates the use of gum paste. Even religious votive objects were made using the method. A ceramic sugar mould of St. Catherine of Siena, dating from the late fifteenth or early sixteenth century, excavated on the site of the Old Bailey, survives in the Museum of London (plate 3).

In Europe, the method was occasionally used to create large-scale pieces, most notably in Rome in the seventeenth century, but a great deal of skill was required to get an acceptable result and it was much more suitable for making fruits and small figures. Fruits moulded from grained sugar syrup had been served among the sugar sculpture at Italian Renaissance banquets and printed directions to make these start to appear in England from the late sixteenth century onwards. In 1600, Sir Hugh Platt describes moulds carved from wood as well as those cast from actual fruit in 'burnt alabaster' (plaster-of-Paris). These were usually three-part moulds and were soaked in water before use. Sir Hugh tells us how a sugar pear, or lemon, could be cast in a mould of this kind. After the sugar had been boiled to the correct 'height', he tells us to take off:

'the cappe of your molde, poure the same therin, filling up the molde above the hole, and presse it downe upon the Sugar, then swing it upp and downe in your hande, turning it rounde, and bringing the neather parte some times to bee the upper part in the turning, and è converso'.

This agitation of the mould evenly coats its inner surface with the syrup, which eventually candies into a hollow fruit. Moulds of sulphur, lead and pewter were also used for this work. Sugar boiled to the 'correct height' or feathered degree (about 240°F) was poured into the damp mould, which had previously been bound tightly with tape, and the mould rotated a few times to coat the inside with a thin layer of sugar. Any waste syrup was poured out through the opening. When the sugar had cooled, the mould was opened to reveal a perfect life-size orange, lemon or pear in hollow candy. A convincing finish was given to the fruit by painting it with food colours. In the nineteenth century the little brown spots on pears were achieved by painting them with *a decoction of coffee, chocolate, and Spanish-liquorice juice*, while the bloom on peaches was supplied by dusting them with fine powder sugar. *Trompe l'oeil* artificial fruits were also moulded in ice cream, marzipan and *pastillage* paste. Those made of marzipan were even dipped in isinglass jelly to produce a soft, yielding, touch and finished off with a lifelike bloom of starch.

The Venetian Connection

It is likely that both gum paste and cast sugar came to be used in Italy at a very early period as a result of the strong trading links that Venice and Genoa enjoyed with Byzantium. During the medieval period, most of the sugar that came into Europe passed through the hands of Venetian merchants, as did many Levantine botanical materials such as tragacanth. Marzipan is another edible modelling material with traditional, though tenuous, links to Venice. Its name is said to be derived from the Latin *Marci panis*, meaning the bread of St. Mark, though this derivation is not entirely convincing. It was certainly being made in France as early as the thirteenth century. It was made from a combination of ground almonds (sometimes pistachios) and sugar, bound with egg white and is a coarser material than gum paste. It is thought to have been used in the medieval period for creating the sculptural centrepieces known as *entremets*, *sotelties* or *warners*, which were frequently displayed at courtly meals. However, when *sotelties* are mentioned in descriptions of medieval feasts, their mode of production is rarely described and it is quite likely that many were modelled from wax and other more orthodox materials. When Ann Boleyn was crowned Queen in 1533, her feast in Westminster Hall featured *'subtleties and shippes made of waxe, marvylous, gorgeous to behold'.*

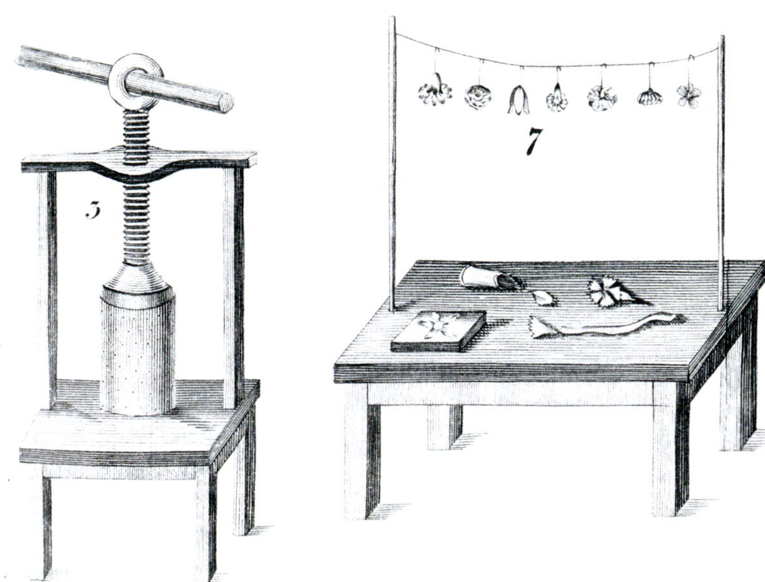

Plate 4 (see page 11)
A press for forcing gum tragacanth paste through linen and a stand rather like a miniature washing line for drying sugar flowers. Illustration from G. Jarrin, *The Italian Confectioner*, London,1820.

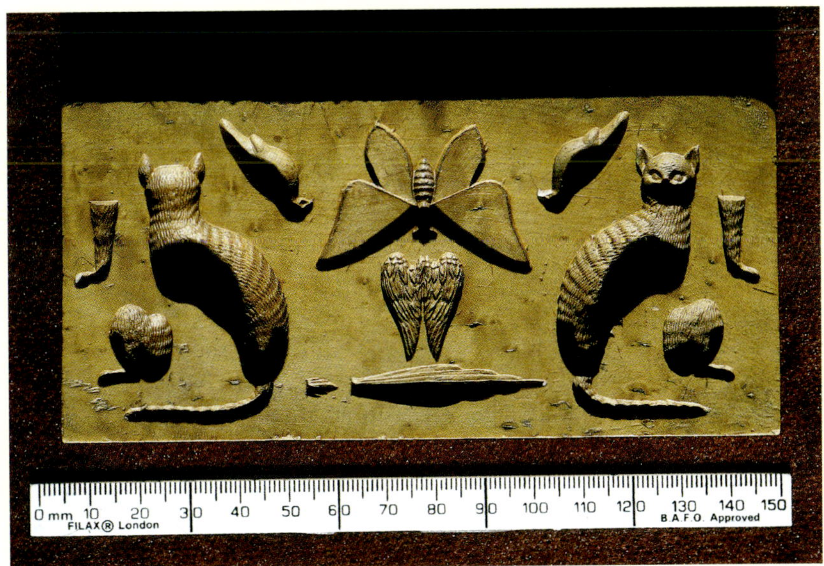

Plate 5 (see page 11)
Detail of boxwood mould carved with components to create a sugar-paste cat. French, 1820-30. The Bowes Museum, Barnard Castle, Co. Durham.

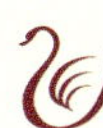

During the seventeenth and eighteenth centuries, artists and confectioners further developed all these methods of creating edible table ornaments. Detailed designs for sugar sculpture start to appear in French and Italian works during this period, but rarely are there any full accounts of the methods used to construct these extraordinary objects. Both professional confectioners and artists seem to have been keen to preserve their trade secrets. A French *officier* (confectioner) called Gilliers, who describes himself as the confectioner to the deposed King of Poland, offers some remarkable plates of gum-paste table ornaments and confectioners at work, in *Le Cannameliste Françoise*, an encyclopaedic work published in Nancy in 1750. However, the author does not discuss sculptural techniques in detail in the text.

It is not until the early nineteenth century that a confectioner actually revealed the secrets of the sugar ornament maker's trade to the general public. This was Gugliamo Jarrin, who had once made sugar sculpture for a reception in Paris for the Emperor Napoleon. After the Battle of Waterloo, Jarrin became ornament maker at James Gunter's confectionery shop in Berkeley Square in London, where he had been *'in the habit of mixing sixty or eighty pounds of gum paste every week'* to provide wealthy Mayfair households with sugar table decorations. In his book *The Italian Confectioner* published in London in 1820, Jarrin tells us that, when making such a large quantity as this, he would use a special press for forcing the sugar and gum mixture through a linen cloth to render it fine and pliable (plate 4).

We learn also that there were different grades of gum paste. Fine paste was made from good quality gum tragacanth and sugar only, and was used for making ornaments that might be eaten. Common gum paste had a large proportion of starch added and was used in the trade to mass-produce figures and other decorations that were not for consumption. In Jarrin's time, cheap moulded figures and animals made from common paste were imported from Germany and France in considerable quantities. Non-edible ornaments were also made from pastes of rice flour and the powders of plaster, alabaster and marble, all using tragacanth as the binding agent.

Some figures, animals and birds were directly modelled in fine sugar paste, and according to Jarrin were without dispute, much better than those made in a mould, as the modeller can give a grace and attitude to his figure, which it is impossible to obtain from the other mode. The furry coats of animals like sheep were obtained by providing a texture with a notched goose quill to simulate *'the frizzled appearance of the wool'*. Sculptures of any size made with gum paste also had to be constructed over a wooden or metal armature.

As most confectioners' modelling skills were limited, simple figures, fruits, sugar baskets and many other decorative features were pressed with gum paste out of wooden and plaster moulds. These were often carved or moulded by the confectioner himself. Figures and animals were generally made in two halves and then joined back to back, the limbs and wings often being pressed separately and attached later (plate 5). Jarrin tells us that moulds could be made from imported sugar figures. These were left in a cellar, or other damp place, so the two halves could be easily separated and then cast in plaster. These ornaments were either left in their plain white condition, or were painted with pigments ground with gum arabic. A little sugar was added to make the colour shine. They were also sometimes sealed with a varnish made from gum arabic, egg white and sugar.

The wooden moulds described by Jarrin would have been chiefly of fruitwood or boxwood and carved in intaglio. They had been an important element of the European confectioner's equipment since medieval times. A sixteenth century York cook called William Thornton left an impressive variety of these 'prints' in his will of 1551. They included:

'a print called Sampson: print with Fleurdelice; small leache print, print with Lion and Unicorn; standing print with hart and hind; print with one knot; close print with birds;....print with other arms on it; small print; print with wheatsheaf; print with dolfinge'

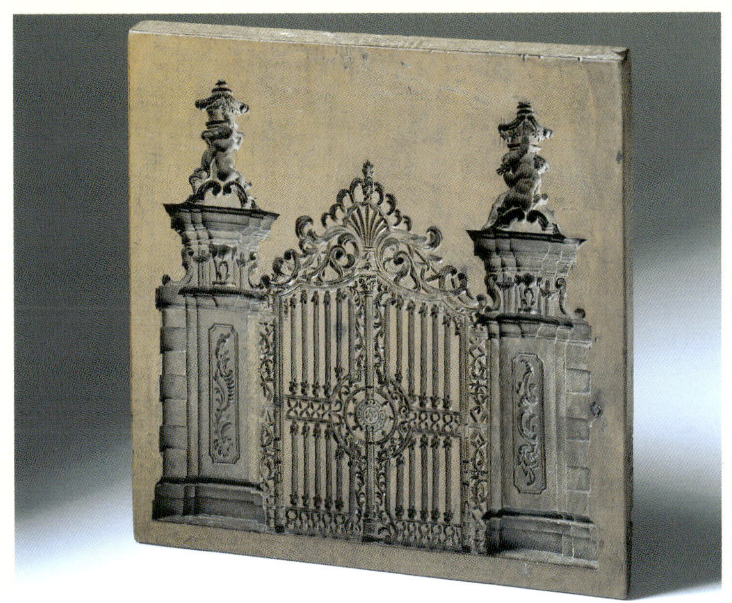

Plate 6 (see page 13)
Carved wooden mould,
first half of the eighteenth century.
Bayersiche Verwaltung der staatlichen.
Schlösser, Gärten und Seen, Munich

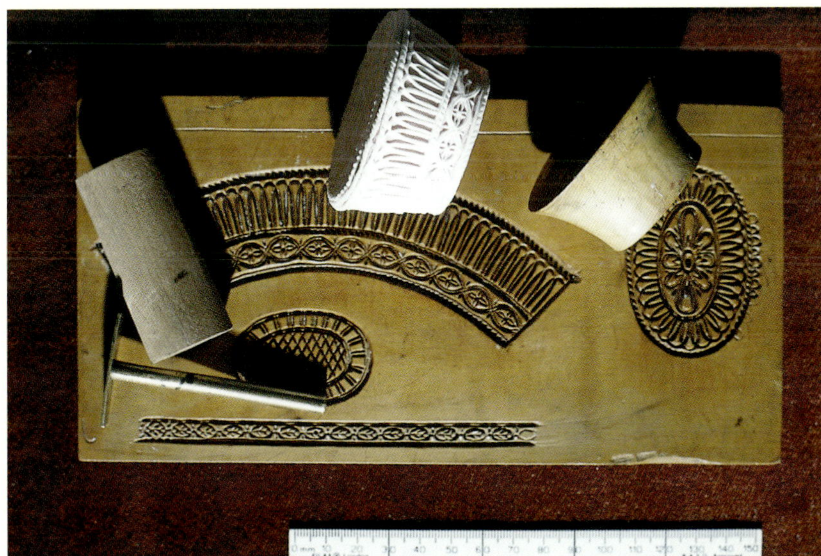

Plate 7 (see page 13)
Basket mould with form and scrapping tools, together with a sugar basket made using the mould. French, early nineteenth century. The Bowes Museum, Barnard Castle, Co. Durham.

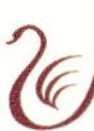

Card Moulds

Confectioners who worked in aristocratic households often had access to a large number of moulds to construct and ornament elaborate centrepieces. These were sometimes in the form of a *card*, consisting of a wooden block carved on both sides with a number of components. These could be separately pressed out of gum paste and then assembled to create a small three-dimensional sugar object. A mould of uncertain provenance (possibly Dutch or English), c.1720, survives in the Pinto Collection in Birmingham Museum and Art Gallery, which can be used to construct a tiny tester bed. Historian Maureen Cassidy-Geiger has recently discovered a number of card moulds in Dresden and Munich dating from the first half of the eighteenth century (plate 6). One of these enables the confectioner to construct a hay wagon, complete with tiny sheaves, rakes and flails. The tines of the rake are carved down the side of the mould to facilitate easy removal.

Multi-part moulds for constructing pierced sugar baskets have also survived. While still pliable, the sides of the basket were flexed around wooden forms and then allowed to set hard. These are always on a very small scale and were probably used as containers for bons-bons, jewel fruits and other sweets. A unique set of early nineteenth century basket moulds, together with their matching wooden forms are displayed in the exhibition (plate 7). These appear to have belonged to a contemporary of Jarrin called Prati. Remarkably, pierced baskets made with sugar paste from these moulds are actually finer than any contemporary examples made from porcelain. The smaller ones resemble fine lace, rather than porcelain.

Finely carved moulds were expensive. In 1809, the Edinburgh based confectioner Caird tells us that a *'board of various figures, such as leaves, flowers, trophies, etc. will cost about 3L'.* In England, confectioners frequently refer to moulds of this kind as *mosaics*. They were particularly suited to creating detailed ornamentation for applying to iced cakes and miniature sugar architecture. After the moulds and sugar paste had both been lightly dusted with starch from a small linen or silk bag, the paste was pushed into the carved impressions. Excess paste was removed by running the blade of a flat knife across the surface of the mould. This was also accomplished with a small boxwood baton, which was used like a squeegee. With very fine work, such as pierced-work baskets, a specialist brass scrapping-tool was used to shave off excess paste. By banging the mould on the table, the resulting shock caused the sugar impressions to pop out, though they sometimes needed to be persuaded to do this with the tip of a knife. Jarrin suggested that frequently used moulds should be bound in iron to prevent them from splitting through continuous knocking out.

Little animals, birds and figures made up from separate parts needed particular attention when assembling. Fine wires were used to support limbs and other vulnerable details. Jarrin describes the process:

'Small Animals, in fine paste... are commonly made with double moulds, giving the back and front representations of the objects, which are afterwards to be joined together. You must push the whole quantity of fronts you would have, and place them in order on boards, or very smooth plates, that they may dry perfectly straight; taking care, when you push them, to put pieces of fine wire in the legs, &c., as they are apt to break. The next day you push the backs, which you must loosen gently in the mould; put the dry front to it, which touch with some liquid paste inside, that it may stick to the other; take it out, and with a modelling tool, join it exactly, smoothing it off with a hair pencil, dipped in water colour them afterwards to your taste'.

Sugar sculpture could either be left plain white, or painted with colours made by grinding pigments with gum arabic and a little sugar to make the colour shine. Red was made from cochineal or carmine, green from spinach, beet or buckthorn, yellow from saffron or gum gambodge, blue from Prussian blue and black from burnt ivory. When sugar sculpture was intended to be eaten, the colours used were of plant or animal origin. However, when they had a purely ornamental purpose,

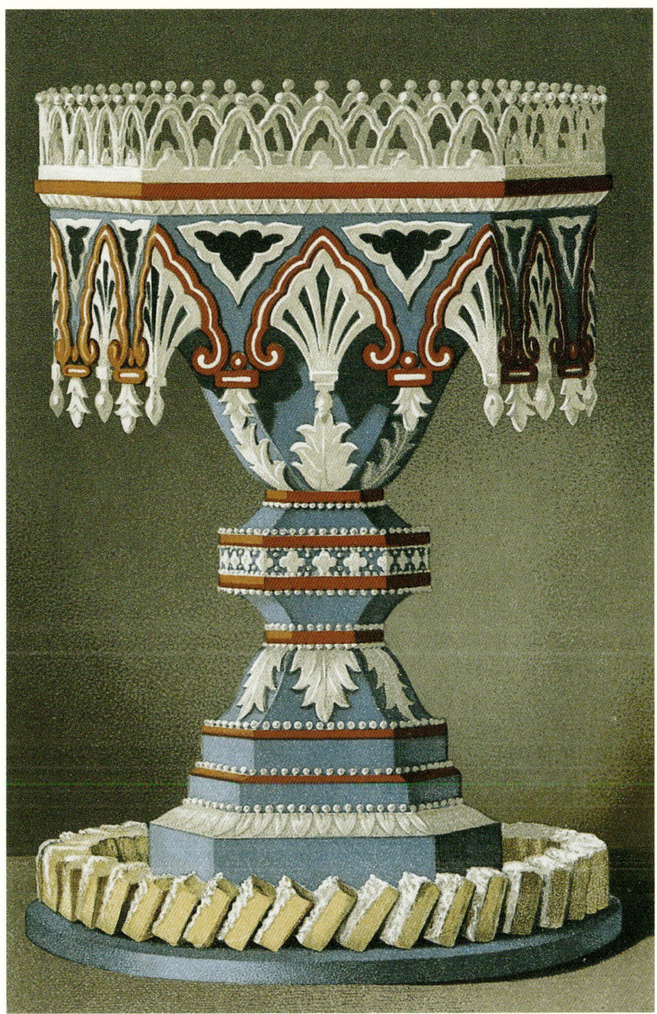

Plate 8 (see page 15)
Pièce montée in the form of a Moorish stand. Decorative items not intended to be eaten were sometimes painted with oil colours. Illustration from Jules Gouffe, *The Royal Pastrycook and Confectioner*, London,1868. (Private Collection).

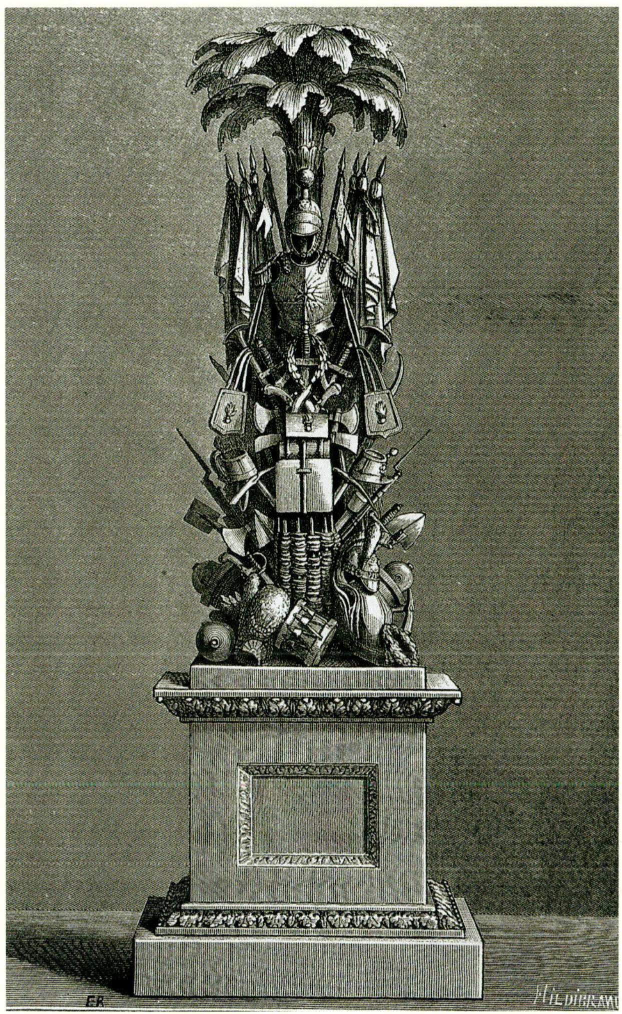

Plate 9 (see page 15)
Design for a military trophy. This illustration is accompanied by instructions for making both this ornament and a similar naval trophy. The author tells us to mould them from green sugar paste and then to gild them, creating a finish like that of weathered bronze. From Jules Gouffe, *The Royal Pastrycook and Confectioner*, London, 1868. (Private Collection).

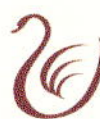

dangerous mineral colours were sometimes used. In the 1860s the French confectioner Jules Gouffe recommended proprietary oil paints for colouring inedible and ornamental *pièces montées* and sugar work (plate 8). These decorations were frequently gilded and various techniques were used to accomplish this. One was to employ a size made from gum arabic and sugar, which was painted on the areas to be gilded with a fine pencil (paint brush) and left to dry. The confectioner then breathed onto the work and the moisture in his breath made the gold size just tacky enough for him to apply the gold leaf. When a bronze finish was required for statuary, the models were made from green sugar paste and then gilded. Any green that showed through gave the effect of weathered bronze (plate 9).

In addition to carved wooden 'prints', moulds of stucco, sulphur, plaster, pewter and even lead were used for 'pushing' sugar paste and marzipan. During the nineteenth century, culinary mould retailers also sold multi-part moulds of tin and copper, which could be used to construct complex table sculpture, not only of sugar and marzipan, but also from nougat, ice and even ice-cream. Queen Victoria's *chef de cuisine* Francatelli describes a mould marketed by Adams and Sons of the Haymarket, which could be used to create an ice *socle* (stand) in the form of two entwined dolphins. The Parisian firm, Le Tang Fils, illustrate a number of *pièces montées* moulds of this kind in their various catalogues. Some consisted of up to eight parts and could be used to construct complex architectural structures surmounted by *putti* (plate 10).

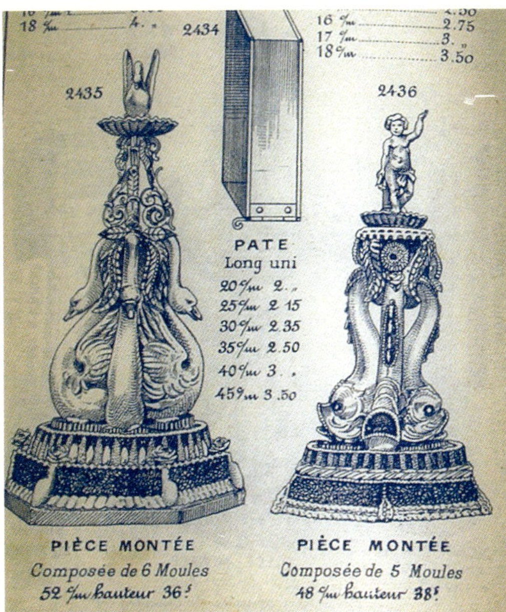

Plate 10 (see page 15)
Designs for *pièces montées* moulds from a trade catalogue published by Le Tang Fils of Paris, late nineteenth century. (Private Collection).

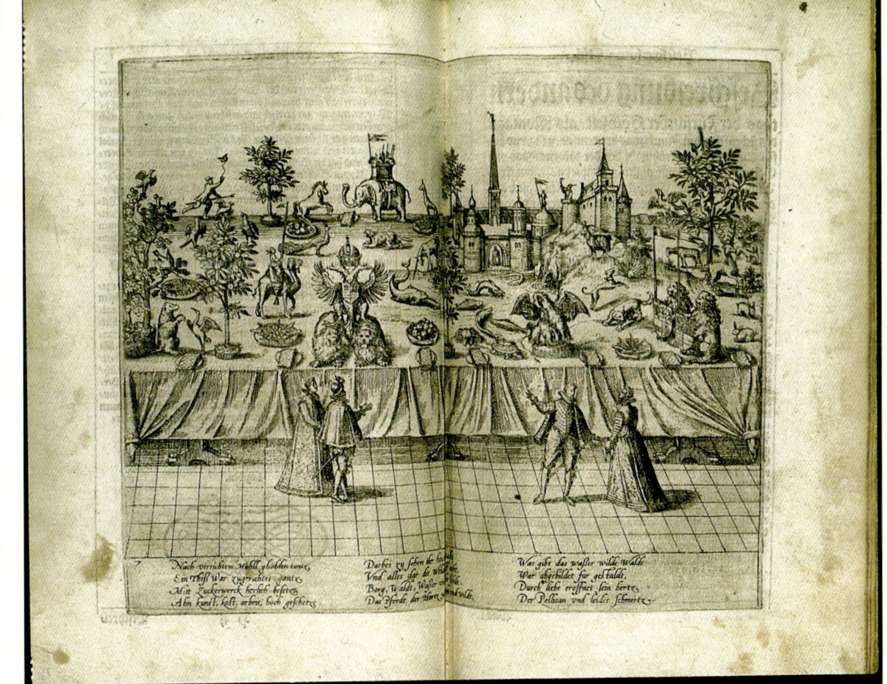

Plate 11 (see page 21)
Wedding feast of Johann Wilhelm, Duke of Jülich and Jacoba of Baden in Düsseldorf in 1585, Franz Hogenburg (before 1540-1590). Etching from Theodor Graminaeus, *Beschreibung. . .*Cologne,1587. (Private Collection)

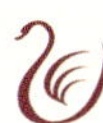

Entremets and sotelties

Sugar sculpture in the late medieval period

Medieval French and Burgundian feasts consisted of a number of buffet-like courses known as *mets*. Sometimes at important state occasions, set piece entertainments took place between each *met*. In their simplest form these so-called *entremets*, involved the prominent display of a piece of sculpture with a particular significance for the occasion. This was usually of a religious, allegorical or political nature. More rarely, much more complex pageants, known as *entremets mouvants*, took place between each course. These sometimes involved costumed performers (or even automatons) and a host of carpenters, painters and sculptors were employed to stage them. Jaques Daret, (a follower of Robert Campin) and Hugo van der Goes were among the many artists who designed and produced spectacles of this kind at the wedding feast of Charles the Bold and Margaret of York at Bruges in 1468. During one of the many spectacular *entremets mouvants* at the feast, a dwarf riding on a lion presented Margaret with a flower (a marguerite in honour of her name) and sang to her an allegorical song composed by Antoine Busnois. As sister of Edward IV, Margaret would have been familiar enough with the protocol of entremets, though at the English court they were known as *sotelties* or *warners*.

English court *sotelties* were based on the French model and, like them, usually consisted of a piece of allegorical sculpture accompanied by a related text or poem. Reserved for occasions such as coronations and wedding feasts, they (like all medieval art) were intensely religious in nature. At an English bridal feast, more or less contemporary with that of Margaret's extravaganza in Bruges, the first course was accompanied by a sculpture of a lamb with the text, *'I meekly unto you, sovrayne, am sente, to dwell with you, and ever be present'*. That of the second course was *'an antelope sayng on a sele that saith with scriptour, beith all glad & mery that sitteth at this messe and pray for the king and all his'*. An angel with the verse *'thanke all, god, of this feste'* featured in the third course. The *soteltie* of the fourth and final course was appropriately a *'wif lying in childebed, with a scriptour'*.

Very rarely the subject matter contained references to themes from classical antiquity. The first course *soteltie* at the wedding feast (after 1414) of Hugh Courtenay, Duke of Devonshire (1389-1422) was a sculpture of Ceres, one of the earliest recorded uses of a pagan deity in English art. Brightly painted and gilded, these creations probably resembled the polychrome wooden and alabaster sculpture of the period. Though marzipan (and more rarely sugar) were used in their construction, it is likely that wax was the most frequently employed material.

The Coronation Feast of Henry VI

Although it could in no way compete with the Bruges wedding feast later in the century, one of the most colourful of medieval English court entertainments was the Coronation feast of Henry VI in Westminster Hall on November 6th 1429. Henry, the only son of Henry V and Catherine of Valois, had become King on the death of his father in 1422 when he was only nine months old. After the death of his French grandfather Charles VI, the English declared Henry King of France, in accordance with the Treaty of Troyes (1420). However, the French would only recognise Charles VII, son of Charles VI, as their legitimate monarch. After the defeat of Joan of Arc, Henry was crowned King of France in Paris in 1431.

Henry's Westminster coronation feast vividly demonstrates how the medieval soteltie could be used not only as an instructive tool, but also as a potent form of political propaganda. Three courses were served to the King at this remarkable meal, each followed by a *soteltie* in the form of a group of figures. The *soteltie* of the first course referred to the implicit saintliness and legitimacy of the English royal line, as well as their prowess in battle. It included the figures of

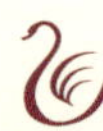

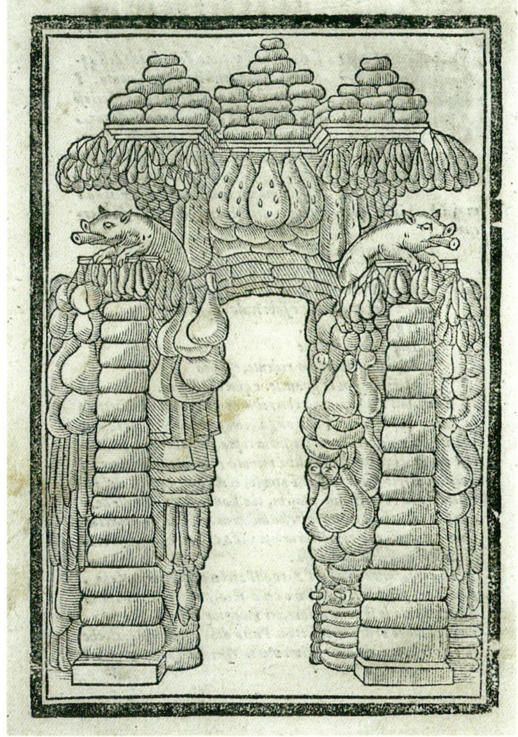

Plate 12 (see page 23)
Macchina della Cuccagna in the form of a triumphal arch made from parmesan cheeses, salame, hams and suckling pigs. This was constructed in 1629 in honour of Duke Antonio Alvarez di Toledo, Viceroy of Naples.
Woodcut from Francesco Orilia, Il Zodiaco, Naples, 1630.
(Private Collection)

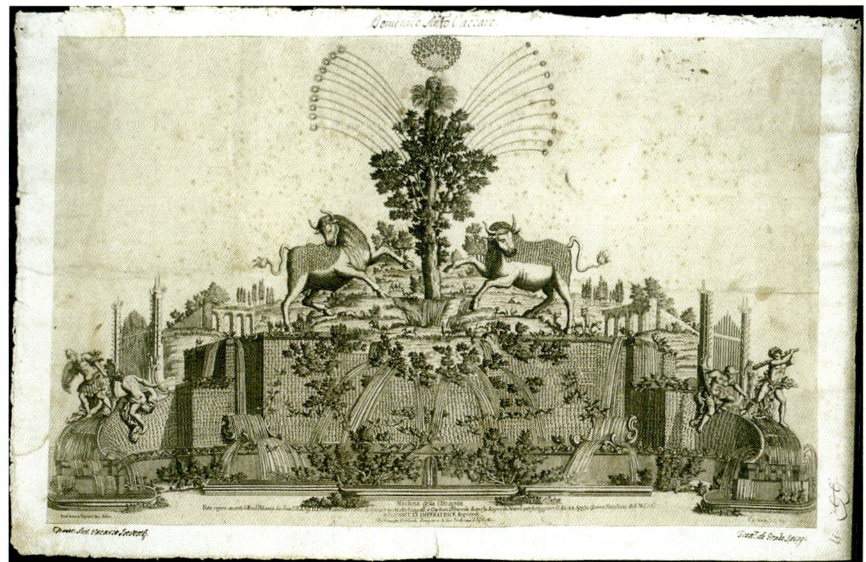

Plate 13 (see page 23)
Macchina della Cuccagna. Naples,1720-1730.
This monument, made entirely from food, was constructed to celebrate the birthday of the Empress Elizabeth Christina. It was designed by the set designer Michele Angelo de Blasio (active first half of eighteenth century). Etching. Francesco de Grado (active first half of eighteenth century) (Private Collection).

'Seynt Edwarde and Seynt Lowys armyd' as well as the young King Henry in his armour. The first two lines of a text under the feet of the saints read:

'Holy seyntes, Edwarde and sent Lowyce
Concerve this braunche, born of your blessyd blode'.

The second course *soteltie* consisted of figures of the Holy Roman Emperor Sigismund and the King's father Henry V. These were intended as models for the young King of a monarch's role as a *'noble knyghte'* fighting for *'Christes cause in actes marcyall'*. Sigismund had fought the Ottoman Turks (albeit unsuccessfully) and Henry V had defeated the Lollards at home and the French against all odds at his famous victory of Agincourt:
'Agayne myscreants the emperour Sygysmunde,
Hath shewyd his myght, whiche is imperyall.
And Henry the V. a noble knyghte was founde,
For Christes cause in actes marcyall
Cherysshed the churche, to Lollers gave a fall,
Gyvynge example to kynges that succede
And to theyr braunche here in especyall,
While he doth reygne to love good and drede'.

The final and most revealing sculpture was:

'A sotyltie of our Lady, syttynge with her childe in her lappe, and she holdynge a crowne in her hande. Seynt George and seynt Denys knelynge, on eyther syde, presentyd to her Kynge Henryes fygure, berynge in hande this balade, as foloweth:
O blessyd Lady, Cristes moder dere,
And thou seynt George, that called art her knyght;
Holy Seynt Denys, O master most entere,
The sixt Henry here present in your syght
Shedyth, of your grace, on hym your hevenly lyght;
His tender youth with vertue doth avaunce,
Borne by discent, and by tytle of ryght
Justly to reygne in Englande and in Fraunce'.

Political motives were also expressed in many of the other food items before the young monarch. Some of these were decorated with allegorical and heraldic emblems in gold leaf, such as the first course *'Custarde royall with a leoparde of gold sytttinge therin, and holdynge a floure delyce'*. Among the many second course foods was a *'frytour'* garnished with a leopard's head in gold and two ostrich feathers. The third course included a *'bake mete'* in the form of a shield *'quartered red and white, set with losynges gylt, and floures of borage'*. This colourful spectacle must have appealed greatly to the young King, who was only eight years old at the time.

Sotelties continued to be features of important court and ecclesiastical meals during the sixteenth century when sugar and marzipan seem to have taken over increasingly from wax as the modelling materials of choice. Cardinal Wolsey seems to have frequently used them to impress visiting foreign dignitaries. Wolsey's biographer George Cavendish relates a feast prepared for the reception of the French ambassadors at Hampton Court in 1527:

'there were Castelles wt. Images in the same, powlles Chirche & steple in proporcion for the quantitie as well counerfeited as the paynter shold have paynted it uppon a clothe or wall. There were beastes, byrdes, fowles of dvers kyndes And personages most lyvely made & counterfet in dysshes, some fighting (as it ware) wt. swordes, some wt. Gonnes and Crosebowes, Some vaughtyng & leapyng, Some dauncyng wt. ladyes, Some in complett harnes lustyng wt. speres, And wt. many more devysis than I am able wt. my wytt to discribbe. Among all oon I noted there was a Chesse bord subtilly made of spiced plate wt. men to the same, And for the good proporcyon bycause that frenche men be very experte at that play my lord gave the same to a gentilman of fraunce commaundyng that a Case shold be made for the same in all hast to preserve it from peryssshyng in the conveyaunce therof to hys Contrie'.

Unfortunately, no contemporary illustrations of these events have survived in English records. However, a German illustration of a table with sugar figures, for the marriage of Johann Wilhelm, Duke of Jülich and Jacoba of Baden in Düsseldorf in 1585, gives us a rare insight into how

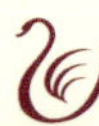

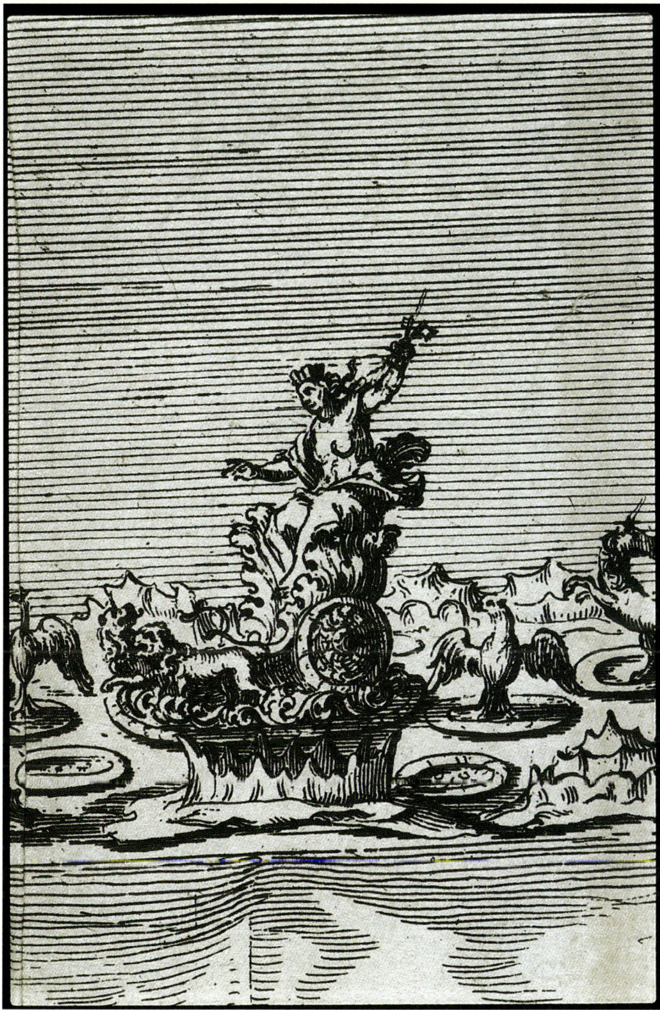

Plate 14 (see page 27)
Detail of large folding plate from John Michael Wright, An Account of his Excellence Roger, Earl of Castlemaine's Embassy, London, 1688. Engraving. Arnold van Westerhout (1651-1725) after Giovanni Battista Lenardi (1656-1704). (Private Collection).

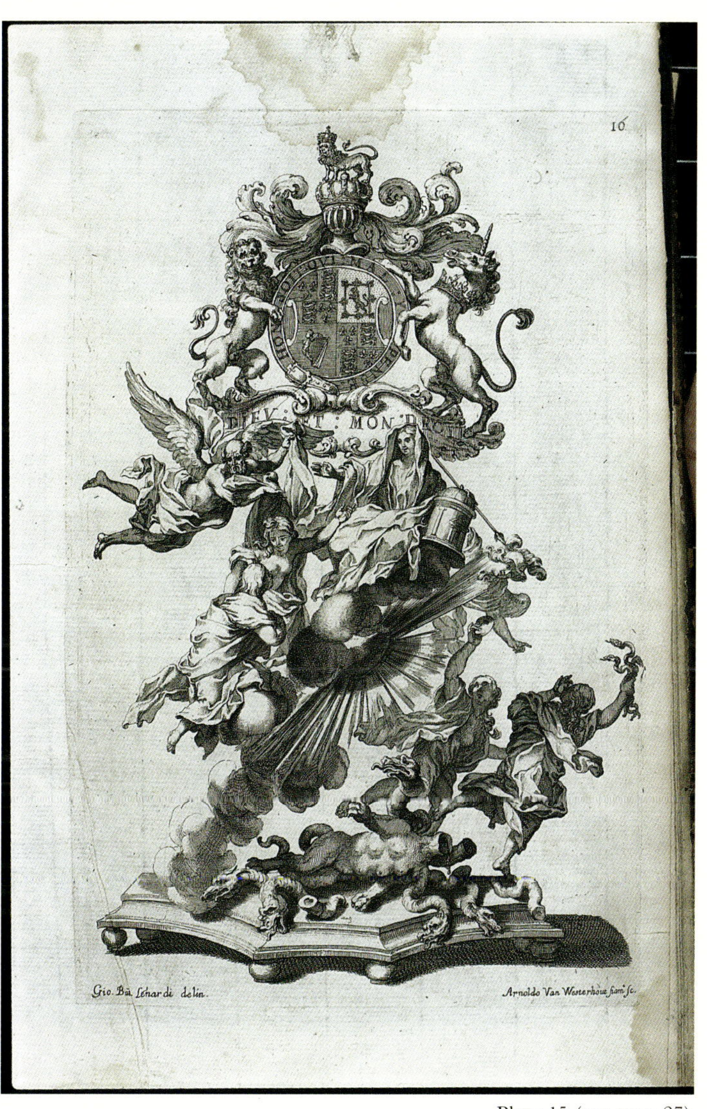

Plate 15 (see page 27)
The *macchina* in the centre of Palmer's table. Engraving. Arnold van Westerhout (1651-1725) after Giovanni Battista Lenardi (1656-1704). (Private Collection).

extraordinary these displays of artistry must have looked in the sixteenth century (plate 11).

A Gift of Sugar for Elizabeth I

Sugar models of *powless Chirche & steple in proporcion* (St. Pauls Cathedral) seem to have become a royal Tudor tradition. In 1562, the surveyor of the cathedral presented Queen Elizabeth with a four-foot high example. By her reign, the medieval court tradition of displaying the *sotelties* at the end of each course was becoming rather old fashioned. Instead, elaborate sugar work and conceits tended to appear after the meal had been consumed. This 'after-course' was an amplification of the medieval *issue de table* or *void*, when wafers, comfits and spiced wine were consumed in ritual fashion before the monarch washed his hands and left the table. In England, this precursor of the modern dessert became known as the *banquet* course and was frequently consumed in a purpose-built building called a banqueting house. The *sotelties* of the earlier Tudor period became known as *conceits* or *standards* and were frequently mounted on large marzipan bases known as *marchpanes*. As sugar became more widely available, the comfits and wafers of the void were augmented with a host of other sweet foods, many of them of southern European origin, such as marmalade, quince paste and *biscotti*.

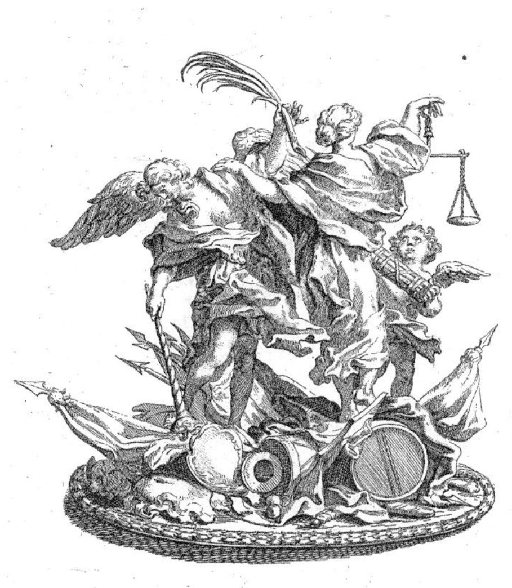

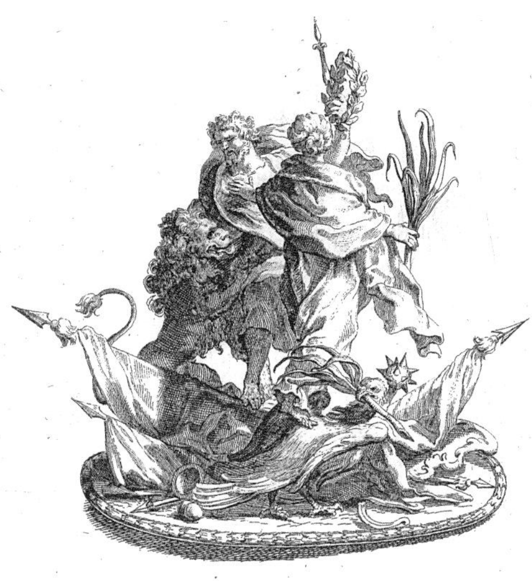

Gio Batta Lenardi delin. Arnoldo V. Westerhout fiam.° sculp

Plate 16 (see page 27)
Sugar sculptures of Justice and Valour.
Engraving. Arnold van Westerhout (1651-1725) after Giovanni Battista Lenardi (1656-1704).
(Private Collection).

et 12

Gio. Batta Lenardi delin. Arnoldo V. Westerhout sculp

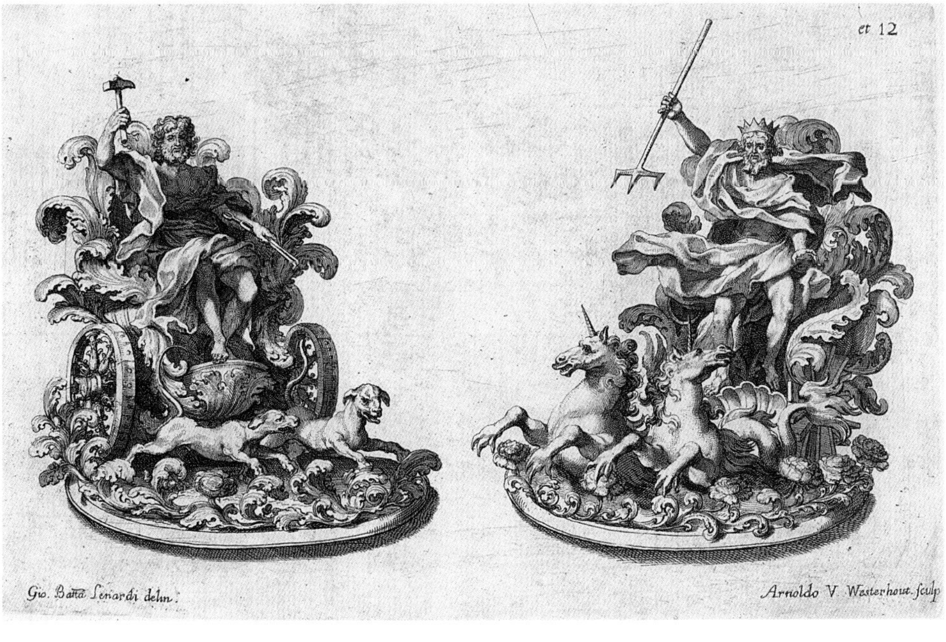

Plate 17 (see page 27)
Sugar sculptures of Vulcan and Neptune.
Engraving. Arnold van Westerhout (1651-1725) after Giovanni Battista Lenardi (1656-1704).
(Private Collection).

Trionfi di tavola

Renaissance and Baroque Sugar Sculpture

The likely model for the enlarged *void* was the ultimate course of the Italian Renaissance *banchetto*. This was served from the *credenza* (sideboard) and consisted of an array of *conditi* and *confettioni* (candies and comfits), frequently served with *stecchi profumati* (perfumed toothpicks). A highly skilled officer called a *credenziere* held responsibility for the production and display of these luxury foods. It was also one of his principal duties to provide, or commission, the creation of suitable sugar ornaments, the so-called *trionfi di tavola* (triumphs of the table).

During the Renaissance, the Italians certainly developed sugar sculpture techniques to a very high level of accomplishment, creating *trionfi* of dazzling design and virtuosity. At very important events, major artists were commissioned not only to produce sugar sculpture, but also to superintend celebratory firework displays and other more unorthodox creative activities. In 1600 the Florentine mannerist artist Bernardo Buontalenti organised the celebrations at the wedding feast of Henry IV and Maria de' Medici for which Pietro Tacca produced the sugar sculpture depicting the absent bridegroom. Buontalenti, who was celebrated for his mechanical genius, contrived a breathtaking array of entertainments for the end of the feast. One of these was a table, which actually moved across the room and transformed itself into two sparkling fountains. The space where the table had stood was filled by a sideboard, which gradually rose out of the floor. This was entirely covered with sculptural *trionfi*, plates, drinking cups and napkins, all made out of sugar paste.

This Tuscan elaboration on the Burgundian *entremet mouvant* may have had its origin in Florentine artists' dining clubs of the late fifteenth and early sixteenth century. The painter Andrea del Sarto belonged to one such society, at which he and his friends amused themselves by constructing edible temples with columns of salami and Corinthian capitals carved out of parmesan. The *entremets* and *sotelties* of medieval Europe north of the Alps, were fundamentally gothic in character, while the *trionfi* of the Renaissance Florentine feast utilised the artistic and architectural language of revived antiquity.

Festivals and Feasts

Many kingdoms and duchies in the Italian peninsula had long had a folk tradition of street festivals in which food was used to construct large architectural tableaux. In medieval Bologna, the *Festa della Porchetta* (feast of the roast pig) featured arches and other architectural fantasies made out of Parmesan cheeses and Parma hams (plate 12). Most spectacular of all were the Cuccagna festivals of Naples and Rome, when huge pavilions and structures entirely made out of food dominated whole city squares. Financed by the king or other local patrician families, these *macchine della cuccagna* were ransacked by the poor and homeless to the amusement of the aristocratic spectators. By the eighteenth century, Neapolitan cuccagna festivals had become large-scale events, for which important stage and opera designers were employed to design and supervise the construction of the annual *macchina* (plate 13).

Cuccagna feasts are well documented, as souvenir prints were sold in the streets to the spectators and many of these have survived, including at least one from the sixteenth century. However, there are very few early images of the *entremets*, *sotelties* and *trionfi* of the courtly table, so we cannot be entirely sure of the true appearance of these Medieval and Renaissance sugar fantasies. We have to depend for our knowledge of these on written descriptions. It is not until the seventeenth century that detailed illustrations of sugar sculpture start to appear in printed accounts of princely

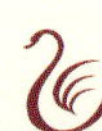

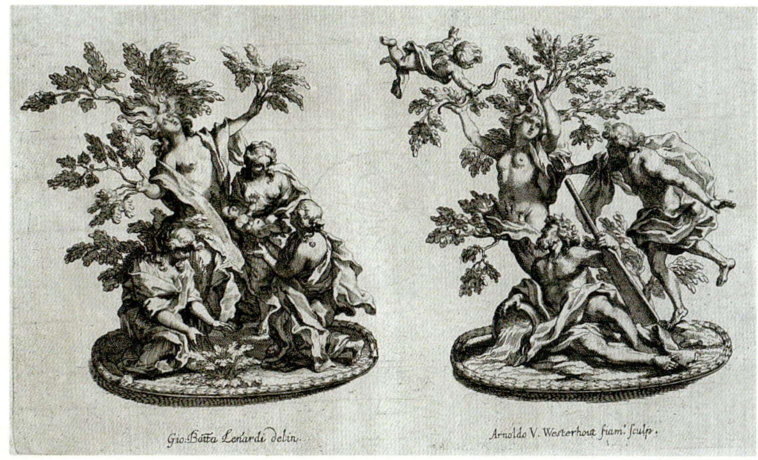

Plate 18 (see page 27)
Sugar sculptures of Myrrha and Daphne.
Engraving. Arnold van Westerhout (1651-1725)
after Giovanni Battista Lenardi (1656-1704).
(Private Collection).

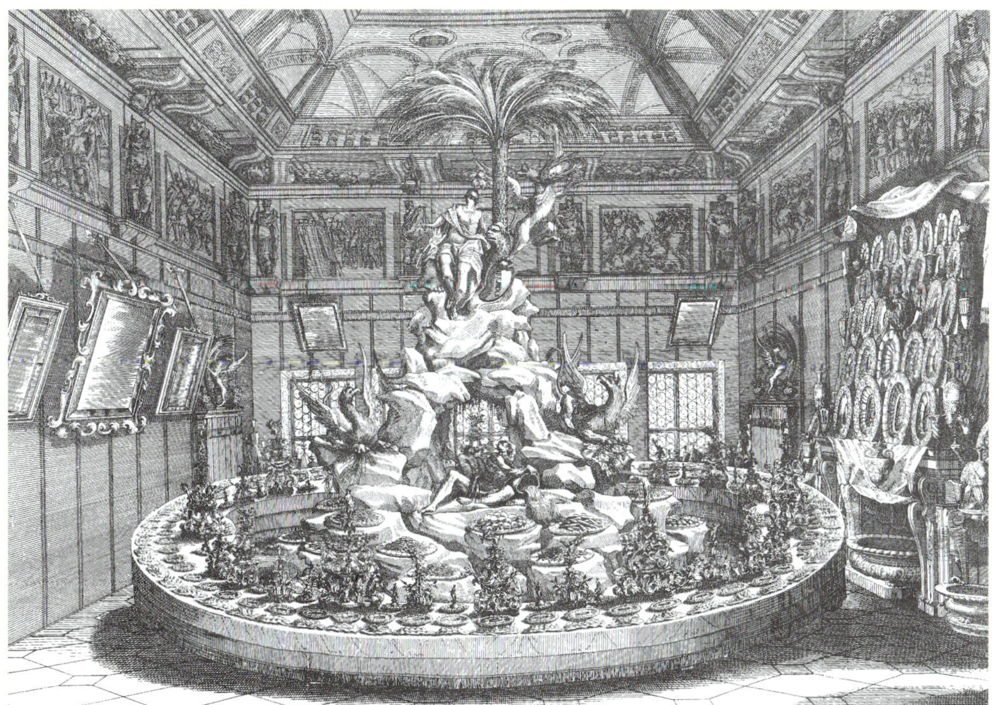

Plate 19 (see page 29)
Table with a *macchina* of *la Felsina*,
protective goddess of the city of Bologna.
Illustration from Francesco Ratta, Disegni
del convito, Bologna, 1693. Etching.
Giocomo Maria Giovannini (1667-1717)
after Marc'Antonio Chiarini (1652-1730).
(Private Collection).

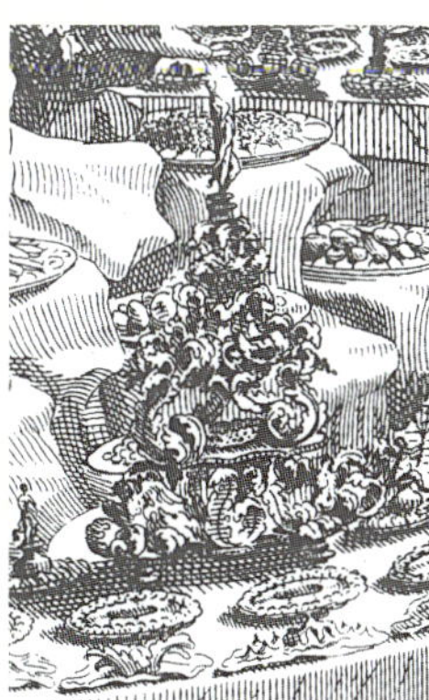

Plate 20
Sugar *trionfi*.

festivals. Like the *cuccagna* broadsides, these books were published as souvenirs for the participants. Many 'festival books' of this kind were printed in the great European centres of aristocratic culture, the most lavish and well known, emanating from the court of Louis XIV, such as André Félibien's *Rélation de la feste de Versailles* printed in Paris in 1676 and illustrated with etchings by Jean Le Pautre (1618-1682). Another account with excellent plates of aristocratic table settings is David Klöcker Ehrenstrahl's *Das grosse Carrosel* published in Stockholm in 1685. This was a lavish production illustrated by Georg Christoph Eimmart (1638-1705), with etchings showing a royal feast celebrating the coming of age of King Charles XI of Sweden.

By far the most important documentation of baroque sugar sculpture is to be found in some albums of sketches by Pierre Paul Sévin, a French artist who lived in Rome between 1666 and 1688. Sévin's drawings are chiefly of papal meals with sugar *trionfi* of an intensely religious character. A feast for Maundy Thursday given by Clement IX in the Vatican in 1667 shows a table decorated with angels carrying the instruments of Christ's Passion, all executed in a lively baroque style. Exactly two years later, Clement celebrated the same feast day at a table dominated by a sugar model of Bramante's Tempietto, a centrally planned church in the classical style, surrounded by *trionfi* of the cardinal virtues.

In Counter Reformation Rome the themes explored by the *trionfi* on the papal table were extremely pious in nature, although more pagan themes were permissible for diners with humanist interests. Catholic aristocrats resident in Rome, such as Princess Rozana and Queen Christina of Sweden, frequently hosted feasts featuring remarkable displays of *trionfi* with classical themes. Sévin illustrates a number of these. One, given in Frascati in 1667 by Rozana for the humanist Cardinal Leopoldo de' Medici, featured a centre-piece representing Mount Parnassus with Apollo and the Seven Muses, surrounded by other mythological figures such as Pegasus and Diana. The Cardinal himself held a reception for Queen Christina which included a miniature sugar copy of Pietro Tacca's monument in Livorno of his ancestor Grand Duke Ferdinand I, surrounded by the famous chained slaves. Many of the trionfi at these baroque receptions in Rome seem to be copies of other well-known monuments and sculpture. It is possible that the same multi-part moulds used to cast editions of miniature bronzes of these popular works were also employed to create versions in cast sugar. When Alexander XII entertained Queen Christina in 1655, soon after her abdication, Ercole Ferrata and Johann Paul Schorr designed the trionfi for the great reception. However, the actual sculptures were cast in sugar at the foundry of the famous Roman bronze caster Girolamo Lucenti. It is possible that extra detail was applied by using gum paste before the statues were gilded with gold and silver leaf.

Alexander XII's feast took place well before Sévin came to Rome, but the artist did attend another papal reception for the Swedish Queen in 1668, given by Clement IX. He produced a watercolour of this event, which shows the Pope and the Queen sitting next to each other at separate tables beneath a great canopy of state. The Pope's table is higher and somewhat larger than that of the Queen. Both are crowded with intricate *trionfi* of gossamer fragility, but the Pope, of course, has many more on his table than the Queen.

A Feast in Rome for James II

During this period, an important reception in Rome for a foreign monarch or ambassador nearly always featured a table or side-board crowded with *trionfi*, usually with an allegorical or political programme, tailor-made for the event. Perhaps the most remarkable of these was a feast given in 1686 by Roger Palmer, the Earl of Castlemaine, who had been sent by James II of England on an embassy to Pope Innocent XI. For over a year, Palmer rented the huge Palazzo Pamphili in the Piazza Navona (now the Brazilian Embassy). The chief purpose of the embassy was to endorse James II's desire to restore Catholicism to England and to get support from the

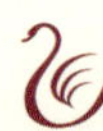

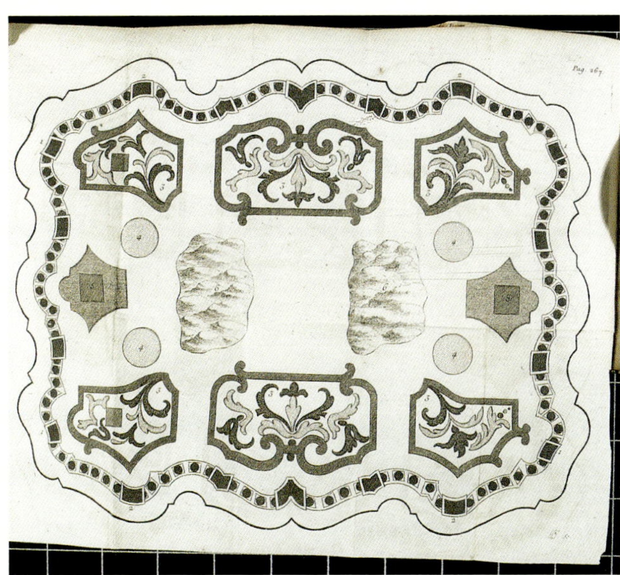

Plate 21 (see page 33)
Plan for a sugar parterre garden for a dessert plateau. Illustration from Menon, *La Science du Maltre d'Hotel Confiseur*, Paris, 1750.
(Private Collection).

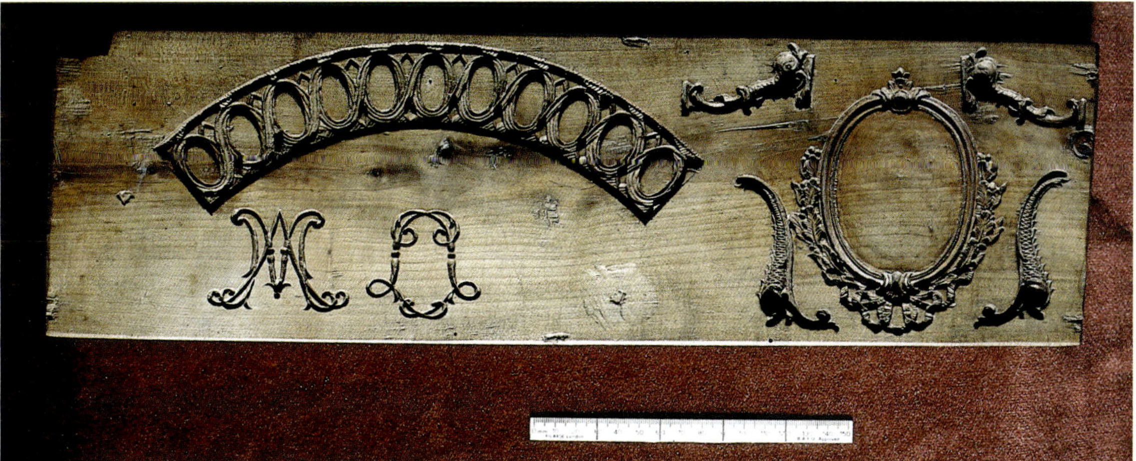

Plate 22 (see page 37)
Hardwood mould with monograms of Louis XVI and Marie-Antoinette with intaglio motif to press a sugar basket. French, late 1780s.
The Bowes Museum, Barnard Castle, Co. Durham.

Pope for a war against the Protestant Dutch. The crowning event of the visit was a reception for eighty-six cardinals, who came to dine in the huge salon on the *piano nobile* (first floor), decorated with frescos by Pietro da Cortona. Palmer's steward, the Catholic portrait painter John Michael Wright organised the occasion. Afterwards he wrote an illustrated work in the European festival book tradition, describing the theatrical display and pomp of the event. This was published in Italian in Rome in 1687, followed by an English version in London in 1688. The illustrations (engraved by Arnoldo van Westerhout after drawings by Giovanni Battista Lenardi) are the most detailed records we have of Roman baroque sugar sculpture. Wright had trained as an artist in Rome and belonged to the city's Guild of St Luke (the painters' guild). He probably had many contacts among the artistic community in the city and may have chosen the painters, sculptors and artisans who produced the equipage for the great feast from his own personal friends. We know that Cirro Ferri designed some magnificent coaches for Castlemaine, but it is not clear who produced the remarkable sugar sculpture for the table.

Wright's book includes a folding plate nearly four feet long, which illustrates the full length of the table (plate 14). Behind the centre of the table, under a great canopy of state hung a life-size portrait of King James painted by Wright. On the table in front of this, was a six foot high *macchina*, the top third of which was decorated with the Stuart Crest. Reminiscent of Bernini's *Cathedra Pietri* (papal throne), the lower part of the centrepiece depicts the rays of the sun appearing from behind a cloud - representing Catholicism emerging from heresy under James' guidance. To reinforce the message, a figure representing the True Church presents Britannia with a model of a centrally planned chapel. Below, a decapitated, multi-headed Hydra, emblematic of Protestant rebellion, is being trampled underfoot by heroes (plate 15). What the fiercely Anglican Whigs back home thought of this is not recorded, but James was forced into abdication not long after the London edition of Wright's book was published in 1688. The huge central *macchina* was probably made from a variety of materials. Wood, stucco and textiles, as well as sugar paste, were all commonly used to construct ephemeral works of this kind.

An impressive range of twelve sugar *trionfi* graced the centre of the massive table, rather like floats in a street procession, punctuated here and there by vases of artificial flowers. Four of them represented the King's virtues - Peace, Justice, Valour and Victory (plate 16). Another group in the form of the Four Elements, demonstrated how the gods Vulcan, Neptune, Cybele and Juno themselves honoured the table and therefore the King, a baroque rhetorical convention frequently used at these events (plate 17). Two sculptures of the metamorphoses of the nymphs Myrrha and Daphne were both strongly influenced by Bernini's *Daphne and Apollo*, now in the Villa Borghese (plate 18). Wright explains the significance of these two works in the text of his book. He informs us that myrrh would not be needed to embalm James' fame in the future, but the laurel would be used to crown his achievements. Two *trionfi* in the form of figures sheltering under palm trees (*phoenix* in Latin), continued the theme of the *macchina*, with its implicit message of the resurrection of Catholicism in Britain. This was also a play on Palmer's name, whose family crest included palm branches. A number of lesser sugar models in the form of lions and unicorns represented the supporters of the Stuart arms, while sugar figures of eagles referred to the Este family *stemma*, the arms of Mary of Modena, James's beautiful young Italian wife. Two days before the meal took place, the palace was thrown open to the public, who were allowed access to the *piano nobile* to admire the sculpture. So great was their curiosity, that Palmer had to call in a company of Swiss guards to ensure that none of the display was looted.

After Palmer's great feast was over, the *trionfi* were not eaten, but given to notable Roman ladies to take home. Presenting sugar *trionfi* to eminent females as gifts appears to have been a well-established tradition throughout Baroque Italy. It also

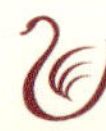

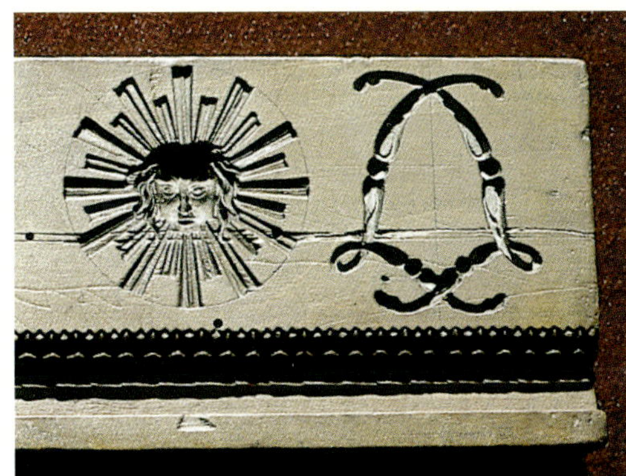

Plate 24 (see page 37)
Monogram of the Kings of France and sun king symbol of Louis XIV. Detail of hardwood mould. French, eighteenth century.
The Bowes Museum,
Barnard Castle, Co. Durham.

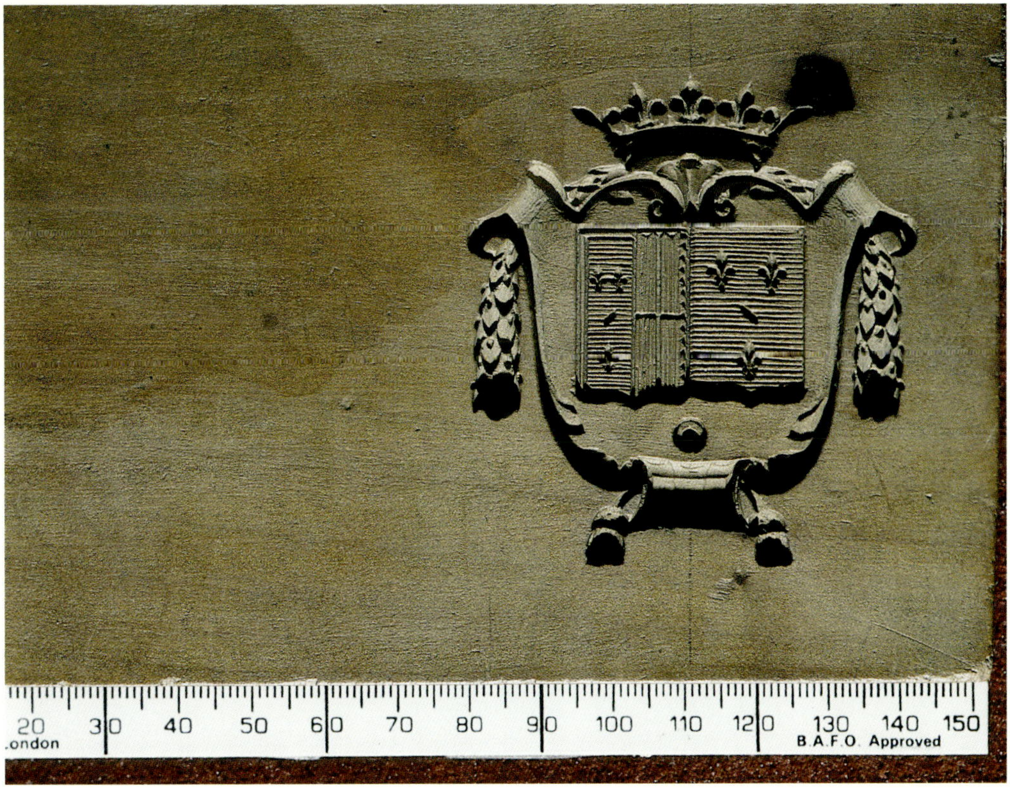

Plate 24 (see page 37)
Mould in the form of the arms of the Princesse de Lamballe. French, before 1789.
The Bowes Museum,
Barnard Castle, Co. Durham.

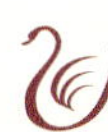

happened after a monumental extravaganza in Bologna in 1693, when Francesco Ratta threw a party to mark the end of his term as *gonfalonier* (city elder). Two festival books were published to mark this event, both of them illustrated with detailed prints of a huge round table dominated by a massive *macchina* surmounted by a life-size figure of *La Felsina*, the protective goddess of the city. This was surrounded with smaller sugar *trionfi* of extraordinary delicacy and great displays of rare fruits and sweetmeats. How the ladies got these gossamer-fine structures home in one piece is not mentioned. Ratta's text indicates that large teams of specialist artisans were hired to stage events of this kind (plates 19 and 20).

In the Italian peninsula, emblematic displays of *trionfi*, lasted well into the eighteenth century. A confectionery textbook, *Il credenziere de buon gusto*, written by Vicenzo Corrado and published in Naples in 1778, illustrates a dessert table for the month of May with sugar allegorical figures of Primavera, Fame and Partenope, the patron goddess of Naples. Corrado also suggests detailed iconographic schemes for the other eleven months of the year. The confectioner had truly become the Michelangelo of the kitchen. Throughout baroque Europe, no aristocratic feast was complete without a finale in the form of a dessert table crowded with goddesses and nymphs. Although the city states and duchies of the Italian peninsula had shaped courtly taste in these matters from the fifteenth century through to the Counter-Reformation, the second half of the seventeenth century saw the growing domination of French court influence on gastronomic trends.

The influence of the lifestyle at Louis XIV's court was enormous. Whether their palaces were in Paris, St. Petersburg, Dresden or Prague, emperors, monarchs and noblemen all adopted the sophisticated French mode of dining. Aristocratic *service à la française* consisted of two buffet-like courses followed by a dessert, frequently served in a separate location. For a while, however, symmetrical arrangements of pyramids of fruit and sweetmeats dominated the centre of the table throughout the meal, a style of dining known as *à la ambigu*. James II's coronation feast in 1685 in Westminster Hall was arranged in this manner, as was that of William and Mary after James's forced abdication.

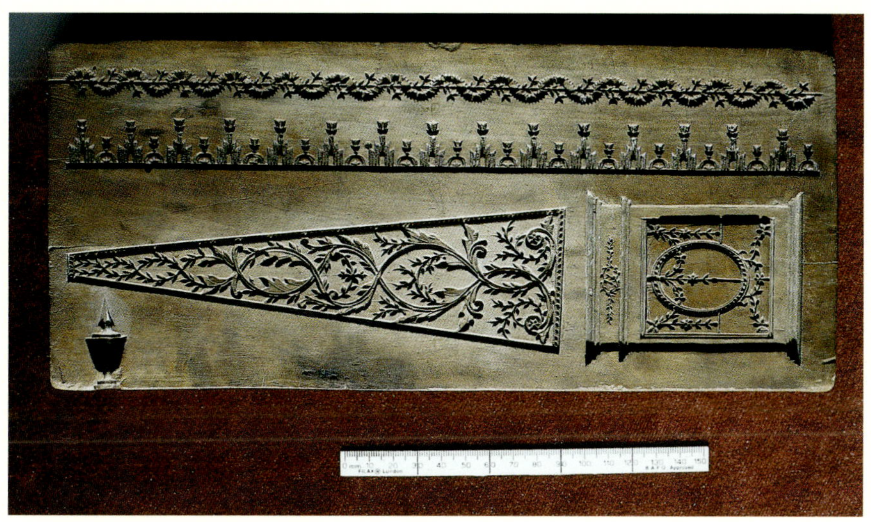

Plate 25 (see page 37)
Hardwood mould with components to create a sugar obelisk.
French, early nineteenth century.
The Bowes Museum, Barnard Castle, Co. Durham.

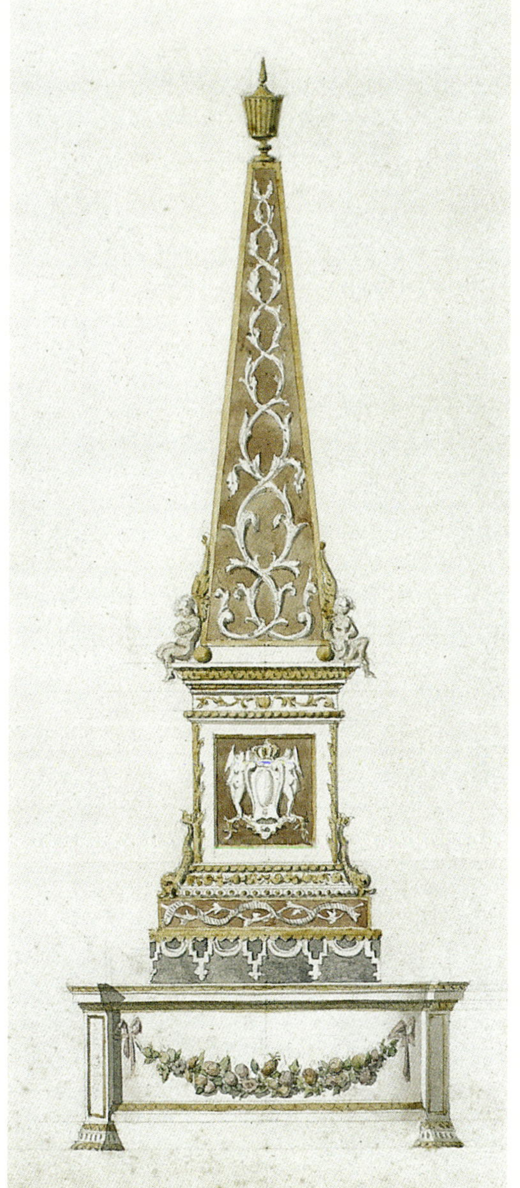

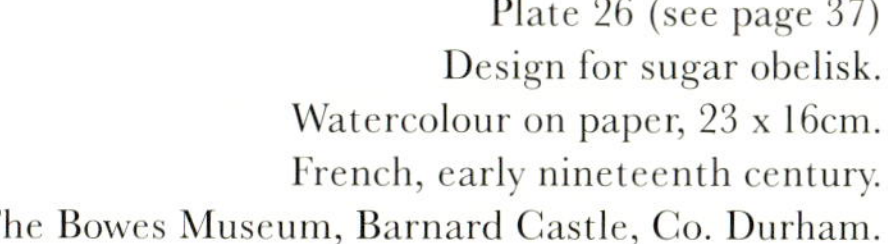

Plate 26 (see page 37)
Design for sugar obelisk.
Watercolour on paper, 23 x 16cm.
French, early nineteenth century.
The Bowes Museum, Barnard Castle, Co. Durham.

Sugar Sculpture and Porcelain

Rococo and Neo-classical Sugar Sculpture

The early eighteenth century saw the sugar sculpture of the dessert having a profound influence on other decorative art forms. These changes seem to have initially taken place at the court of Augustus the Strong in Saxony. According to surviving inventories of the *Hof-Conditorei* (royal pantry), the Dresden court started to use porcelain figures as substitutes for sugar ornaments soon after the foundation of the first European porcelain manufactory at Meissen in 1710. Rare oriental porcelain had been the material of choice for serving the foods of the dessert since the early seventeenth century. As soon as the secrets of making this 'white gold' were discovered in Europe, not only did dessert services start to appear, but also sets of porcelain figures for the centre of the table. It certainly made sense to use a more durable material than sugar for the production of these vulnerable objects. Sugar-paste figures were extremely fragile, expensive to make and must have often deteriorated in damp storage conditions.

However, sugar sculpture was not abandoned, and the Saxon *Hof-Conditorei* continued to list wooden moulds for producing ornaments to be used alongside figures in the new fashionable medium. By the second half of the century, most European porcelain manufactories were producing ceramic dessert ornaments, sometimes as complete sets made for important aristocratic patrons.

Table Decorations at the Court of Louis XV

The *Manufacture Royale* porcelain factory sponsored by Louis XV at Vincennes and later at Sèvres, innovated a pure white unglazed 'biscuit' porcelain in the early 1750s, which imitated sugar sculpture perfectly. Like the Popes of baroque Rome, Louis was able to attract major artists to design and model table decorations in this new medium at the Sèvres factory. Many were made from designs by the painter François Boucher and sculpted by Etienne-Maurice Falconet. Strongly allegorical or emblematic arrangements were now out of favour and popular scenes from the theatre, opera and pastoral life dominated the dessert tables of the Versailles élite. Louis' own royal service, produced between 1753-5, was provided with 242 figures and almost 1,000 decorative features such as baskets, urns and balustrades. Manufactories outside France produced similar sets for special events. A white-glazed porcelain plateau centrepiece with sixty figure groups, single figures and vases was made in Vienna in 1768 for the Golden Jubilee of Abbot Rayner I at Zwetyl Monastry.

Brightly coloured bouquets of artificial flowers of silk, feathers or paper, arranged in purpose-made vases and baskets, punctuated the stark whiteness of these porcelain sculpture garden displays. Sugar flowers had also been popular since the previous century and brief directions are given in confectionery texts such as that of Massialot on how to make them. As well as being employed to *'garnish the tops of pyramids of dried fruits, or to be arranged in a basket'*, they were useful for decorating intricately cut almond paste or spun sugar decorations called *croquantes*, which were used to cover compotiers of preserved fruits. By the 1770s it had become fashionable to adorn the margins of the plateau with swags of sugar flowers hung from vases, terms and obelisks. Gilliers illustrates the equipment required to make *pastillage* flowers in a wonderful image which depicts some spellbound children watching a confectioner magically assembling one of these fragile blooms. The jardinières of glazed porcelain flowers made at both Vincennes and Sèvres may give us some idea of the appearance and style of the sugar flowers of this period. These were themselves designed as centrepieces for plateau dessert services. One, now in the Cholmondeley collection, was sold to Lord Bolingbroke in 1756 as part of a complete *surtout de table* with a brass-framed mirror plateau and eight small vases filled with porcelain flowers.

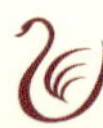

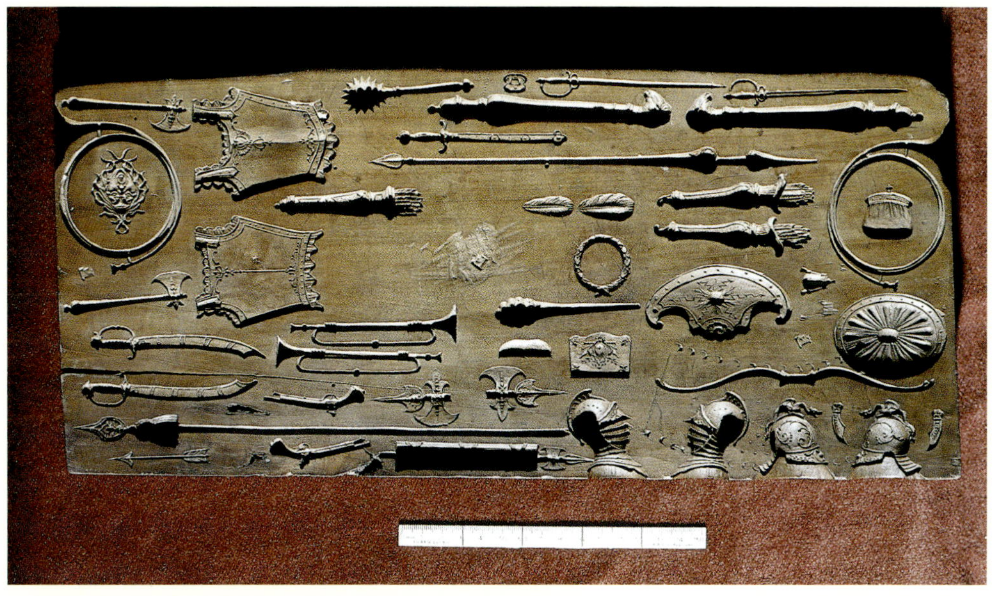

Plate 27 (see page 37)
Mould with components to create a panoply or trophy of arms.
French, late 1780s.
The Bowes Museum,
Barnard Castle, Co. Durham.

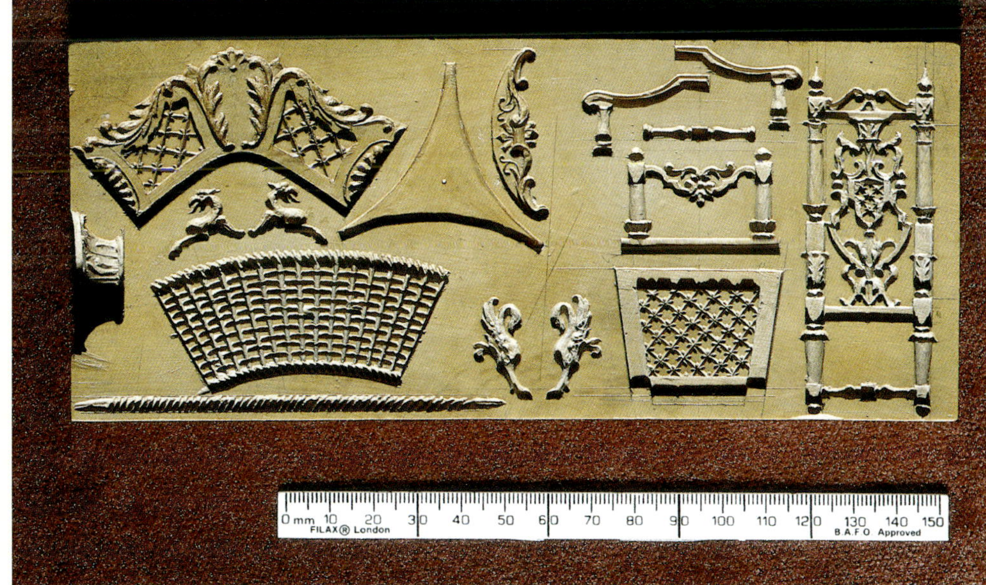

Plate 28 (see page 37)
Boxwood mould with components to create a sugar chair. French, first half of the nineteenth century.
The Bowes Museum, Barnard Castle, Co. Durham.

By this period, a horticultural theme had become the favoured motif for a grand dessert. Well-appointed tables were laid in imitation of formal gardens or parks, complete with flower-beds of coloured sugar, gravel walks made from *dragées* (sugared aniseeds), trees of candy and sugar-paste figures. The *surtout de table*, originally used for holding condiments and *dragées*, evolved into a full-length plateau of looking-glass, on which these decorations were arranged. Between 1740 and 1789 an international craze for this kind of setting, popularised by the Bourbon court, swept through the great cities of Europe. Whether entertaining in Venice or Mayfair, it became fashionable for wealthy hosts to have their desserts laid out in the garden manner. In candlelit palazzi on the Grand Canal, tables sparkled with mirrors covered in swirling parterres, triumphal arches and fountains of brightly coloured Murano glass. In 1765 the Duke of Gordon purchased a complete garden dessert from the Berkeley Square confectioner Domenico Negri. For £25-7s-9d, he was able to entertain his friends at a table decorated with a brass-framed plateau adorned with Bow figures, china swans, glass fountains, parterres, a china umbrella and a kaleidoscopic display of sugar plums and bonbons. A surviving trade card advertising Negri's shop is illustrated with fantasy temples, pagodas and fountains.

The garden setting for a mirror-glass plateau usually featured intricate coloured parterres. These were sometimes made from *mousseline*, a coloured *pastillage* forced through a sieve to produce a mossy material, ideal for making little hedges and borders. They were also constructed from cardboard forms, covered in silk chenille, velvet or baize, which were filled with coloured sugar sands (*sables d'office*) (plate 21). Alternatively, *sables* and tiny *dragées* (*nonpareils*) were sprinkled directly onto the mirror-glass to create flowing patterns round the figures and other ornaments. *Sables* were made by boiling coloured syrup to the feathered degree and stirring it with a spaddle as it cooled. The resulting crystals were put through a sieve to form sands of uniform grain size. *Nonpareils* were made in a balancing pan by gradually coating pulverized orris root particles with sugar syrup until they formed tiny 'hundreds and thousands'. Half a pound of orris root was enough to make almost a hundredweight of *nonpareils*. *Sable* parterres were sometimes also embellished with large crystals of sugar and moulded candy flowers. In the late eighteenth and early nineteenth century, coloured marble dusts were also used to decorate the plateau. Some confectioners had the skill to create pictures of classical ruins and mythological scenes on the plateau. A Hungarian confectioner and portrait painter called Benjamin Zobel became famous for making images from coloured sand when he was table-decker to George, Prince of Wales, the future George IV.

Publication of Designs

Professional French confectioners had started to publish illustrations and do-it-yourself directions to lay out table garden-centrepieces. The first to do so was Menon, whose *La Science du Maître d'Hôtel Confiseur*, published in Paris in 1749, contains detailed etchings of plateau desserts with sugar buildings, balustrades and classical sculpture. The most important of these shows a dessert honouring the sorceress Circe, who through her magical powers turned Ulysses' men into swine. The irony of an allegory of greed would not have been lost on the diners, who had already consumed two or three courses of savoury foods and *entremets*. Publication of designs of this sort tended to codify these table layouts and spread a taste for them far beyond the royal courts (plate 21).

Menon's contemporary, Joseph Gilliers, also published some celebrated plates showing how to lay out a dessert in the most fashionable manner, including one, which illustrates a setting where even the table is in the form of a garden parterre. Gilliers' fantasy table gardens combine standard rococo decorative motifs with chinoiserie elements, which make them more light-hearted than Menon's more formally articulated baroque designs. This was in keeping with prevailing tastes at the court of Louis XV, where a sentimental hedonism prevailed

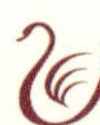

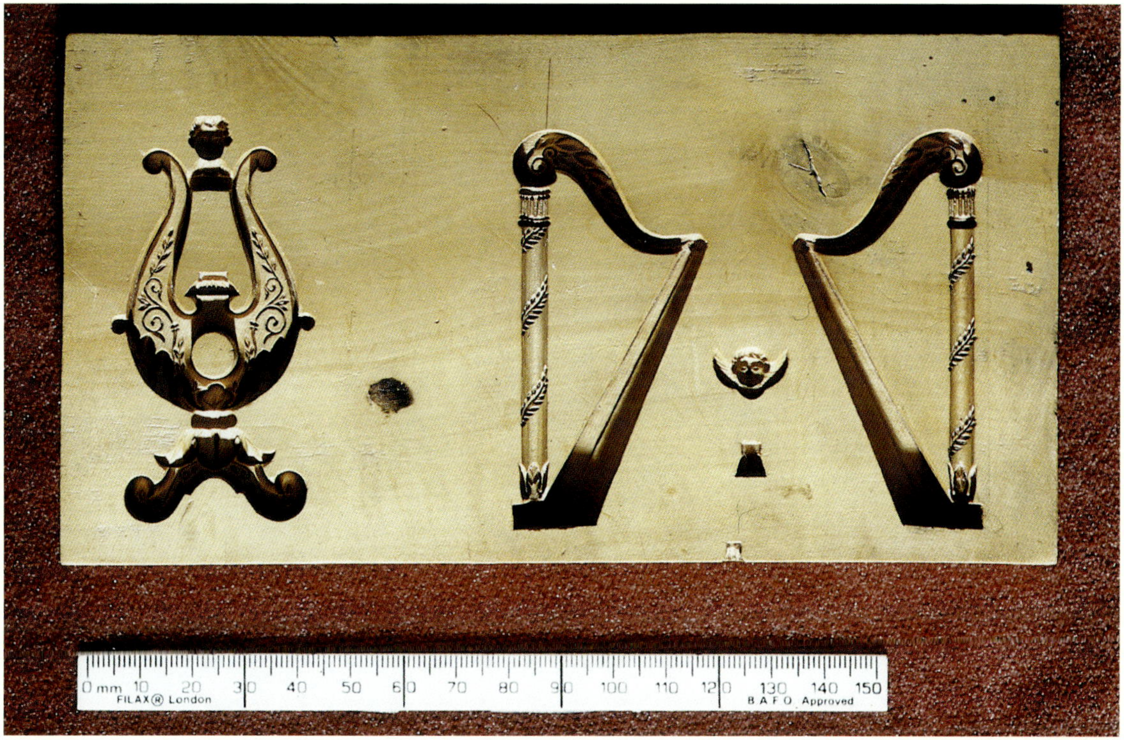

Plate 29 (see page 39)
Boxwood mould carved with motifs to create a sugar lyre and harp.
French, early nineteenth century.
The Bowes Museum, Barnard Castle, Co. Durham.

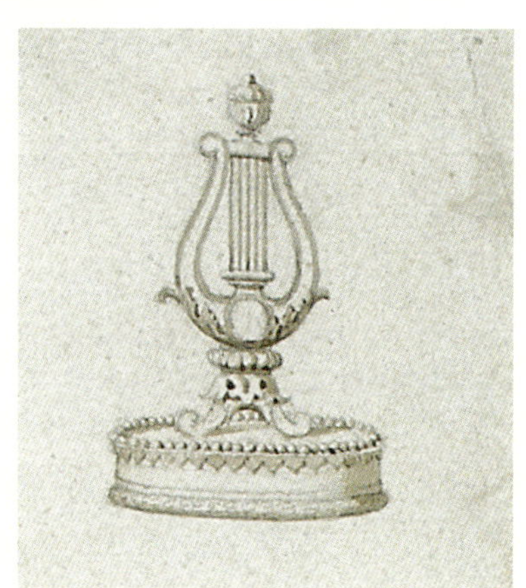

Plate 30 (see page 39)
Detail showing a design for a sugar-paste ornament in the form of a lyre on a decorated stand.
Artist unknown - perhaps Prati (active 1820s).
Watercolour on paper. French, early nineteenth century.
The Bowes Museum, Barnard Castle, Co. Durham.

in the matter of laying out a dessert. Ornamental statuary still dominated the tabletop plateau, but at court, it was more likely to be made from porcelain than sugar paste.

Despite the competition of the porcelain factories, confectioners continued to make table ornaments from sugar paste. Gilliers illustrates designs for some very ambitious rococo centrepieces in the form of fountains and candle holders adorned with Chinese peasants and *putti*. These would have been a challenge to the most skilled confectioner, as sugar paste is a difficult medium. It dries out quickly on the surface, but remains soft within, which encourages surface cracking if the work is moved. Its extreme elasticity also encourages slumping in large freestanding structures, which as a result require the support of wires or armatures. Despite these limitations, it was used to create the most extraordinary ornamental features.

The artistic skills of the eighteenth century French confectioner were legendary. However, since their clientele was exclusively aristocratic, the French Revolution of 1789-93 caused many to leave France and seek employment elsewhere. A few came to London, others went further afield, some crossing the Atlantic and taking with them the art of sugar sculpture to the New World. One exiled Parisian sugar ornament maker, Stanislas Lannuier, sold his wares from a confectionery shop in Broadway, in New York. In 1805, he advertised *'for sale, independent of his sugar-work, a beautiful assortment of ornaments, [including] the Equestrian Statue of Great King Frederick'.*

Military Trophies

At this time, rapidly altering political and social trends were also bringing about stylistic changes in sugar art. The Napoleonic Wars created a militaristic culture, which found its chief gastronomic expression in victory banquets. Confectioners were in great demand, not to create the hedonistic trifles of the pre-revolutionary aristocracy, but to ornament the tables of conquering heroes with magnificent trophies of war. An austere neo-classicism became the visual language of the genre. In 1820, the confectioner Jarrin recollected a piece he had created for a victory reception for Napoleon:

'At a dinner given by the city of Paris to Napoleon, then Emperor of the French, on his triumphant return from Germany, the Author constructed a group, two feet in height; the Emperor, whose figure bore a striking resemblance, was represented standing, and putting up his sword into the sheath, led by Victory, attended by several allegorical figures, which were intended to express the various high qualities so liberally attributed to Napoleon by the French, as long as success attended him. It was made for the centre of a table; and the Emperor, who rarely noticed anything which ornamented the table, observed his portrait, and, with his characteristic attention to works of ingenuity, was pleased to encourage the artist by his approbation'.

In another passage, Jarrin outlined the the skills required by the ornament maker:

'The making of articles in gum-paste is one of the most interesting branches of the confectioner's art. This mode of decoration and embellishment was once in great vogue, and the most magnificent and costly ornaments have been made of gum paste; but it has fallen comparatively into disuse: and, what is worse for the confectioner, the fragments of the art have been transferred to pastry-cooks, and cooks, who have at once disfigured, if not destroyed, the most beautiful flower in the banquet of the confectioner. To make gum-paste properly, great care and dexterity, much patience, some knowledge of mythology, of history, and of the arts of modelling and design, are requisite-qualifications seldom possessed by the mere pastry-cook'.

Jarrin obviously recognised that his art was in decline. The aristocratic patronage enjoyed before the Revolution had vanished and, as a result, the French *officier* (confectioner) was beginning to lose his high social status. His role was being combined with that of the *patissier*, whose position in the kitchen hierarchy had formerly been much lower, closer to that of a mere baker. It is interesting to note that before 1789, recipes for cakes and pastries were not usually included

Plate 31 (see page 39)
Detail showing designs for various sugar ornaments including a crown and turban, both resting on cushions.
Artist unknown - perhaps Prati (active 1820s).
Watercolour on paper.
French, early nineteenth century.
The Bowes Museum, Barnard Castle, Co. Durham.

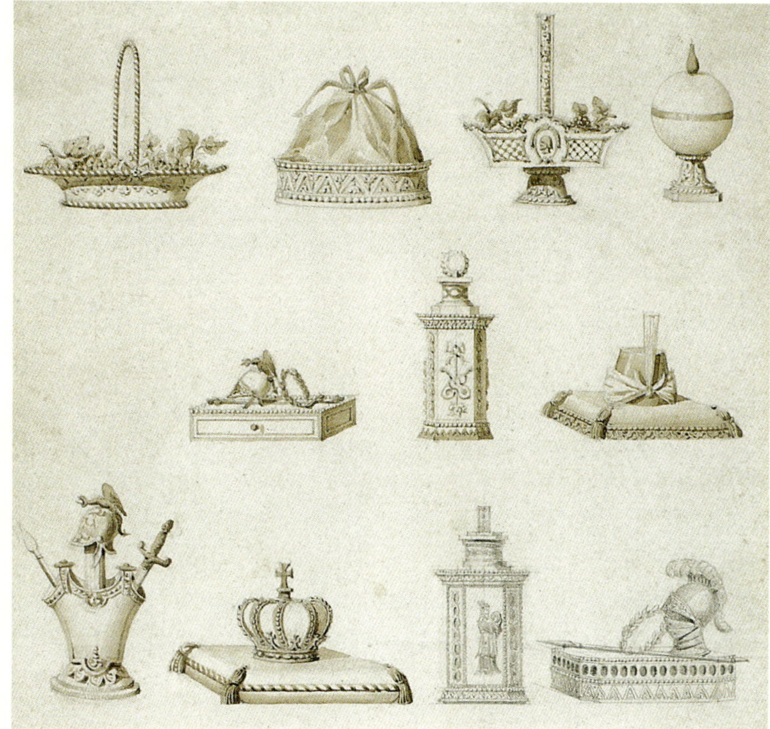

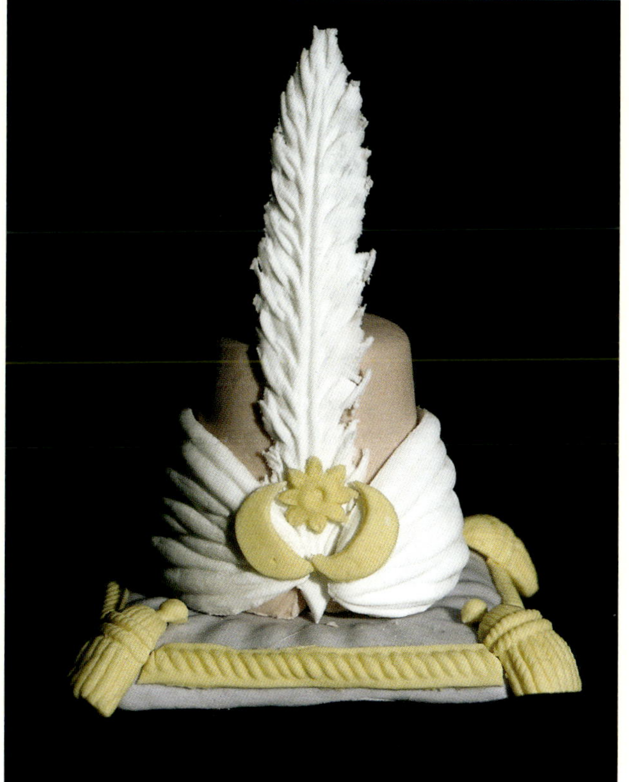

Plate 32 (see page 39)
Miniature sugar turban made from an early nineteenth century boxwood mould.

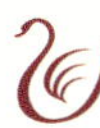

in confectionery texts as their production was not the responsibility of the *office* (confectioner's pantry). This was the case even in England. Frederick Nutt, who like Jarrin, had worked for Gunter's high-class confectionery shop in Berkeley Square, published a little book in 1789. The early editions include no cake recipes, but from 1819 onwards, they start to appear in augmented editions of the book. As the nineteenth century progressed, the roles of the patissier and officier became progressively indistinct.

One of the pastry cooks that Jarrin almost certainly had in mind in his jealous attack was the celebrated Parisian *patissier* Marie-Antoine Carême (1724-1835). This moody and highly creative individual was certainly the most influential culinary professional of the nineteenth century, and his profusely illustrated books codified high-class cookery for the best part of a century. His designs for *pièces montées* and ornamental pastry in the form of classical ruins, Swiss chalets and obelisks, were slavishly copied by his disciples and were still being executed by catering students and competition chefs well into the second half of the twentieth century.

The Bowes Museum Collection

Carême and Jarrin were both at the height of their careers when many of the sugar-paste moulds and confectioner's designs in The Bowes Museum collection were produced. This remarkable assemblage of equipment is probably unique. It consists of forty-seven hardwood boards, many of them carved on both sides on blocks of boxwood, with a total of 730 individual intaglio impressions. Stylistically, most of the moulds appear to date from between 1825 and 1830 and would have been used to create sugar table ornaments of a Percier and Fontaine (French Empire) style. A few are certainly earlier, with motifs associated with the period just before the French Revolution of 1789. One of this distinct group is carved with the royal monogram of Marie-Antoinette, together with an ornamental cartouche and a mosaic to press a late rococo style sugar basket (plate 22). Two others are carved with the intertwined L's associated with the Kings of France (plate 23). A third is engraved with the arms of the Princesse de Lamballe, Marie-Thérèse-Louise de Savoie-Carignan (1749-92), who was a favourite and close friend of Marie Antoinette. She was murdered and mutilated by the Paris mob during the September massacre of 1792. Her body was decapitated and mutilated and her head impaled on a pike in front of Marie-Antoinette's window. It is said that her heart was roasted on a spit and eaten by the mob (plates 1 and 24).

Four of the moulds are signed with the name Duteille, with an address in the Rue de la Consonerrie, Paris, while six others bear the name of Prati. This name also appears on a metal stamp, which has been used to brand the owner's name on the moulds. There is also a boxwood form for constructing baskets, which is stamped with Prati's name. Some of the moulds are partially carved. One has some designs drawn on its blank side, but the carving has not been started. At this period, confectioners frequently carved their own moulds, so it is possible that Prati created some of these moulds for his own use.

Individual moulds survive in many museums and collections, but it is rare to find so many together in such a good state of preservation. To find them with a set of contemporary designs relating to the moulds is unique. There are twenty-seven sheets of pencil drawings and watercolour designs of ornaments.

It is probable that both moulds and sketches belonged to a single confectioner, perhaps Prati himself, who seems to have been in the employ of an aristocratic family, perhaps a branch of the House of Savoie, the family of the ill-fated Princesse de Lamballe. Many of them are of multi-component form, providing the confectioner with a kit to produce a three dimensional object, such as an obelisk or trophy of arms (plates 25, 26, 27). Two allow the construction of some tiny pierced work chairs only six centimetres high (plate 28).

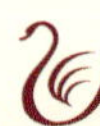

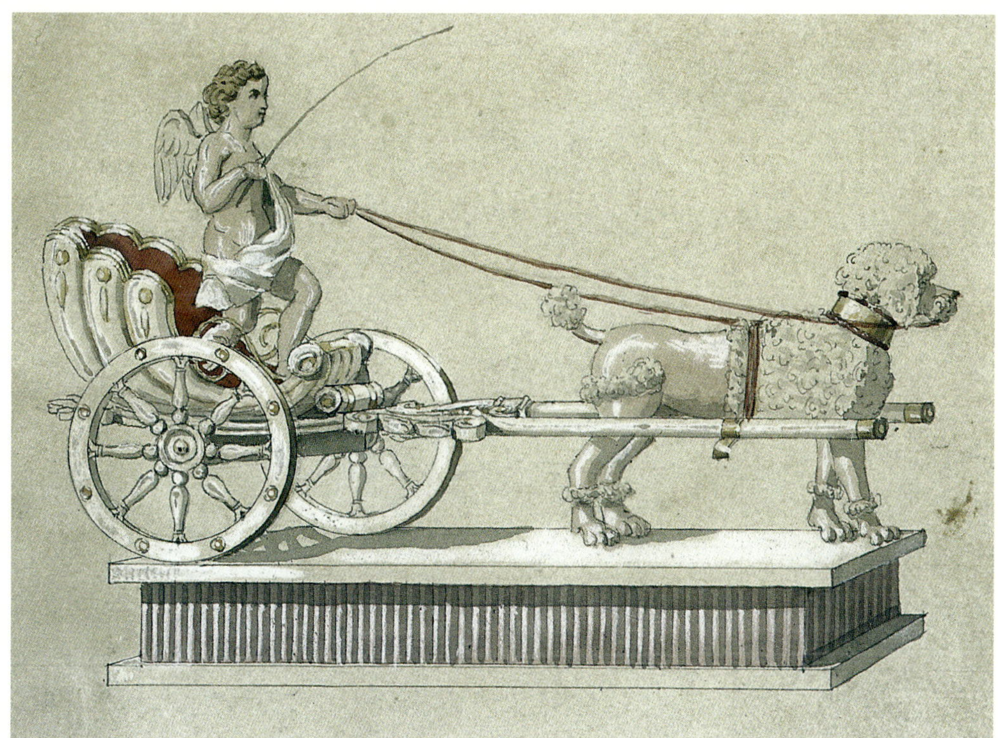

Plate 33 (see page 39)
Design for a sugar ornament of a poodle pulling a triumphal car.
Artist unknown - perhaps Prati (active 1820s).
Watercolour on paper, 10.5 x 13.5cm.
French, early nineteenth century.
The Bowes Museum, Barnard Castle, Co. Durham.

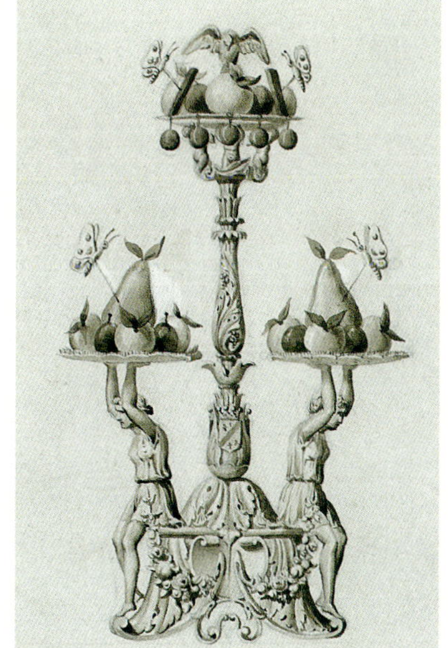

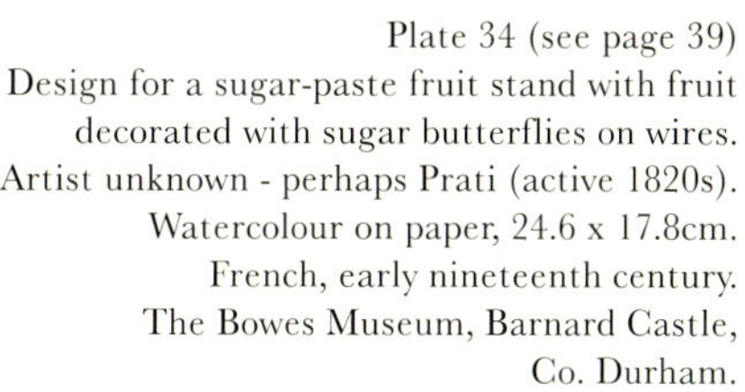

Plate 34 (see page 39)
Design for a sugar-paste fruit stand with fruit decorated with sugar butterflies on wires.
Artist unknown - perhaps Prati (active 1820s).
Watercolour on paper, 24.6 x 17.8cm.
French, early nineteenth century.
The Bowes Museum, Barnard Castle, Co. Durham.

There are also a number of miniature musical instruments: a lute, a harp and a lyre, all of which were designed for mounting on small sugar *socles* (bases) (plates 29 and 30). A mould carved with motifs to allow the construction of two small decorative objects is particularly interesting, as these are both illustrated on a sheet of watercolours. They are a tiny crown and a sultan's turban, both resting on cushions (plates 31 and 32).

Sugar 'Toys'

These miniature sugar objects were known in England as 'toys' and seem to have been popular as ornaments for dessert frames. In 1794, the Prince of Wales purchased *'ornaments for the dessert frames, parterres, coloured marble dust, flowers and balustrades'* from the London based French 'toyman' Louis-Framant Catherine. A sugar toy was located at each place setting, the guests being encouraged to take them home as souvenirs of the occasion. These tiny sugar novelties were also presented as gifts to lady guests and young people at the end of the meal, perhaps a survival of the Italian baroque tradition. At this period, hollow sugar eggs were cracked open by the ladies to reveal presents of small items of jewellery and tiny bottles of perfume.

Carvings of poodles on some moulds relate closely to two of the designs. One of them matches a watercolour of a poodle sitting on a cushion, while another tiny set of carvings relates to a painting of a poodle drawing a triumphal car, though some components of this seem to be missing (plate 33). One illustration shows tiny sugar butterflies on wires impaled in fruits on a stand, creating the spectacular impression of a swarm of butterflies hovering over the table (plate 34). Two very finely carved matching butterflies, identical to those in the designs, survive on a small boxwood mould.

In addition to the poodles, there are other animals and birds - a cat, parrots, dolphins and sea horses - all carved in at least two parts (plate 35). A horse mould has a spare set of limbs, so the pressings can be set up in two different positions). Some components are carved up to the edge of the wooden block to facilitate easy removal, such as a very finely carved military horn on a card mould of trophies.

Some of the most impressive moulds are for creating baskets, frequently with covers and handles. On one board carved with a number of baskets is a miniature wooden bucket. Sugar-paste buckets like this are mentioned in *Soupers de la Cour*, the most important French court cookery book of the eighteenth century. They were used for serving ice-cream, a number of the buckets being filled with the ices and arranged in a larger sugar basket.

A number of moulds are carved with architectural features, such as balustrades, cornices, friezes, capitals and the bases of columns. These would have enabled the confectioner to create miniature sugar buildings, such as a triumphal arch, temple or pavilion. As well as architectural ornaments in the classical style, there are a number of gothic windows with pierced tracery and cusped arches. A large number of moulds are carved with 'fillets' and 'sprigs' in the form of continuous strips of intricate ornamentation used to create impressive borders and applied ornaments for *socles* and pedestals. There are swags, medallions, cartouches and even an entire alphabet.

It is easy to see how a skilled confectioner could construct and decorate impressive ornaments for a special occasion with a set of moulds of this quality. One of the drawings in the collection illustrates a large U-shaped dessert table with a glass plateau covered with pavilions and obelisks. This is also decorated with sable designs in sugar sands or marble dust (plate 36). In order to illustrate this style of layout we have recreated a table setting inspired by this plan.

Trophies for a Kaiser

Throughout the nineteenth and into the early years of the twentieth century, most court confectioners and chefs were inspired by Carême's elaborate approach to presentation. Many of the great chefs had been his students, including

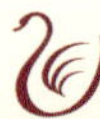

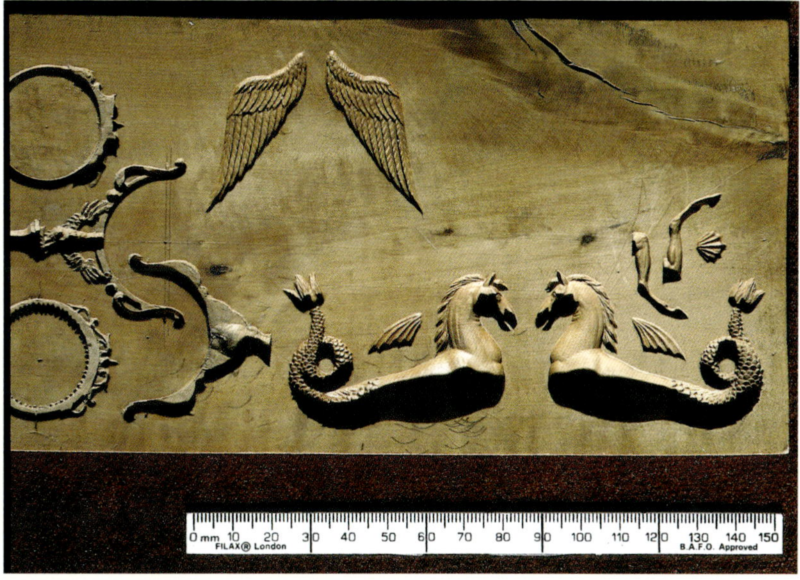

Plate 35 (see page 39)
Boxwood mould with components to create a seahorse with a sculpture of a seahorse made from the mould.
French, early eighteenth century.
The Bowes Museum, Barnard Castle, Co. Durham.

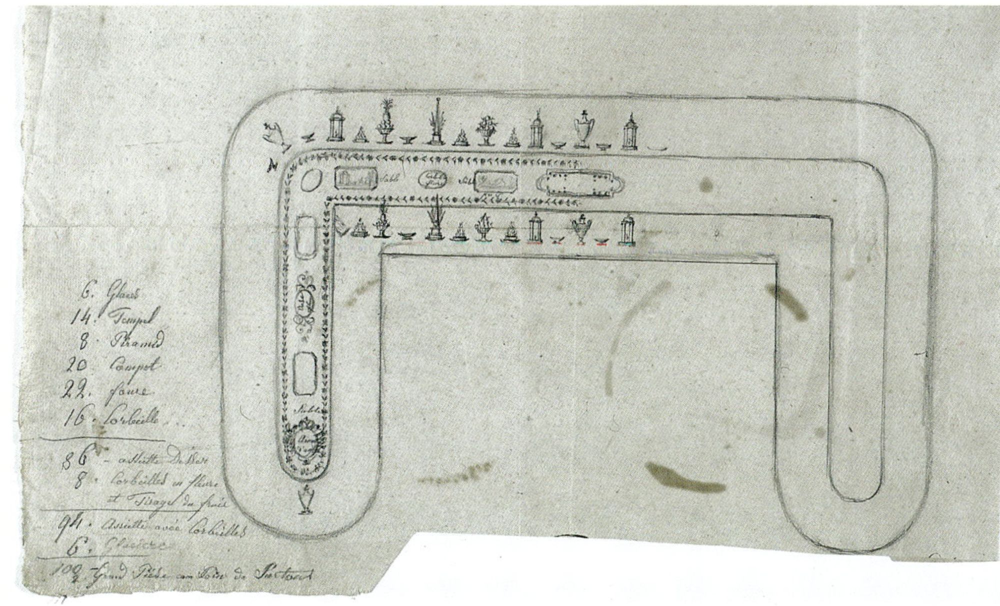

Plate 36 (see page 39)
Table plan for a victory celebration.
Artist unknown - perhaps Prati (active 1820s).
Pencil on paper, 26.8 x 40cm.
French, early nineteenth century.
The Bowes Museum, Barnard Castle, Co. Durham.

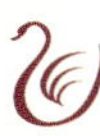

Eustace Ude, Charles Elme Francatelli and Jules Gouffe, who all had a profound admiration for their master. In the entire history of gastronomy, food preparation had never been so complex and mould dependant. As well as sugar paste, every kind of comestible was skilfully transformed into works of art - ice-creams in the form of courting doves, jellies that sliced into royal coats of arms and intricate *socles* moulded from lard. These excesses reached their apogee during the Second Empire of Napoleon III (1852-1871). The most influential chef/confectioner during this period was Urbain Dubois, who together with his colleague Emile Bernard, became *chef de cuisine* to Wilhelm I of Prussia. At Wilhelm's court, the two French masters designed and created intricate foods and sugar sculpture that reflected the Kaiser's two favourite pastimes, hunting and warfare (plates 37 and 38). In their books they illustrated some of their remarkable sugar work and food sculpture (plates 39 and 40). They created gum-paste gothic spires for the emperor nearly two metres high and extraordinary *entrées* mounted on *socles*, moulded from a fine white suet rendered down from the fat around calves' kidneys. These extraordinary structures were constructed on armatures made from pasteboard. The fat was probably pushed into the same kind of wooden moulds that were used for pressing sugar-paste ornaments. The irony is that these two Frenchmen were creating culinary extravaganzas of this level of decadence, for an Emperor who, during the Franco-Prussian war, reduced the population of Paris to eating horseflesh, dogs and sewer rats.

A Remarkable Revival

The social changes brought about by the First World War and the Russian Revolution more or less ended the ancient royal tradition of tables crowded with sugar sculpture. However, the related art of cake decorating continued to flourish in the twentieth century, particularly in Britain and the United States, and a few old-fashioned confectioners continued the tradition of modelling sugar flowers. In some catering colleges, students were encouraged to produce *pastillage* creations for competitions, but by the middle of the twentieth century this ephemeral art had lost both its royal patronage and its sense of direction. At the end of the 1960s, the craft began to undergo a remarkable revival and in recent years has evolved into a worldwide pursuit for both hobbyists and professionals. The universal adoption of the British tiered wedding cake throughout the world has probably helped spread interest in the ancient skills used to decorate this incongruous survival of the medieval *soteltie*. Today imaginative use of the medium results in mixed media sculpture, textured wall works, creations that display humour and quirkiness and works that show superb control of the medium, technical expertise and the attention to detail that would have brought a smile to the faces of the confectioners of past centuries.

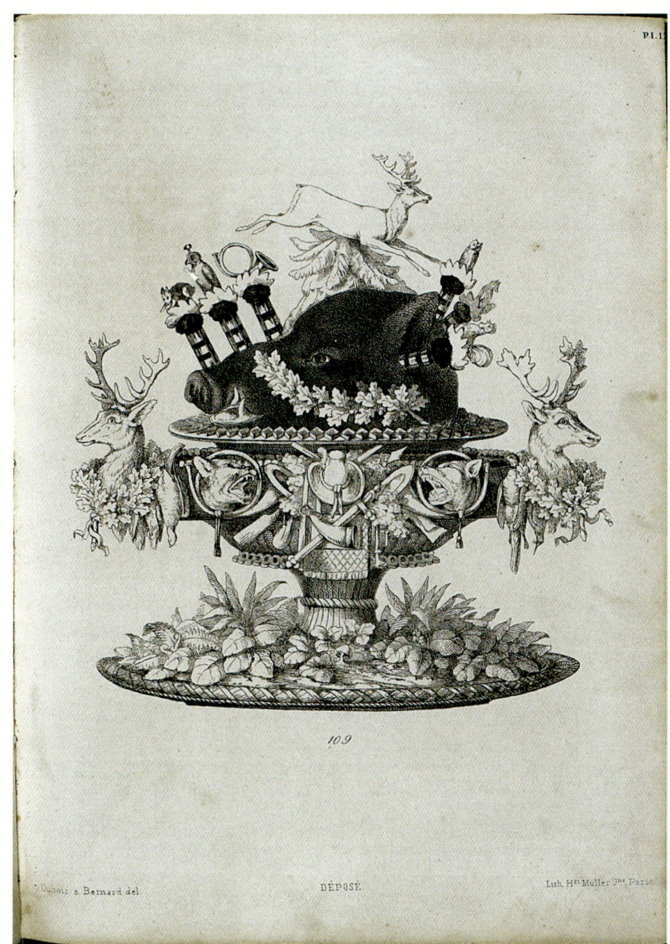

Plate 37 (see page 41)
Boar's head on an ornamental *socle* made from fat.
Lithograph from Urbain Dubois and Emile Bernard,
La Cuisine Classique, Paris, 1864.
(Private Collection).

Plate 38 (see page 41)
Pain de gibier (game loaf) in the form of a fort,
decorated with trophies of war made from fat.
Illustration from Urbain Dubois and Emile Bernard,
La Cuisine Classique, Paris, 1864.
(Private Collection).

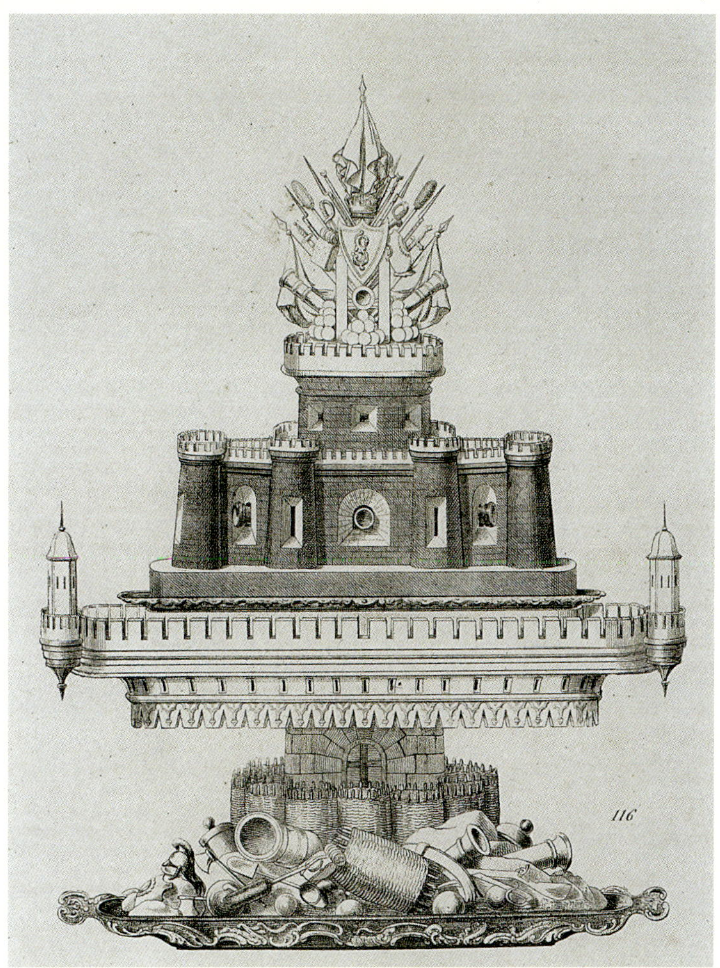

Selected Further Reading

Belden, L.C., *The Festive Tradition: Table Decoration and Desserts in America, 1650-1900*, London and New York, 1983.

Blacker, M.R., *Flora Domestica: A History of Flower Arranging, 1500-1930*, London, 2000.

Bjurström, P., *Feast and Theatre in Queen Christina's Rome*, Stockholm, 1966.

Boucher, B., *Italian Baroque Sculpture*, London 1998.

Brears, P., 'Rare Conceits and Strange Delights', in C.A Wilson (ed), *Banquetting Stuffe*, Edinburgh, 1993, pp. 106-41.

Brears, P., *All the King's Cooks*, London, 1999.

Brown, P. and Day, I., *Pleasures of the Table*, Fairfax House, York, 1997.

Bursche, S., *Tafelzier des Barock*, Munich, 1974.

Catterall, C. (ed), *Food: Design and Culture*, London and Glasgow, 1999.

Chilton, Meredith, *Harlequin Unmasked*, London and New Haven, 2001.

Coutts, Howard, *The Art of Ceramics: European Ceramic Design 1500-1830*, London and New Haven, 2001.

David, E., *Harvest of the Cold Months*, London, 1994.

Day, I., 'Sculpture for the Eighteenth-Century Garden Dessert', in Walker, H. (ed), *Food in the Arts*, Totnes,1999.

Day, I. (ed), *Eat, Drink and Be Merry: The British at Table, 1600-2000*, London, 2000.

Ennès, P., Mabille, G., and Thiébaut, P., *Histoire de la Table*, Paris, 1994.

Fagiolo dell'Arco, M. and Carandini, S., *L'Effimero Barocco*, Rome, 1977-8.

Glanville,Philippa and Young, Hilary (eds.) *Elegant Eating*, Victoria and Albert Museum, London, 2002.

Mason, Laura, *Sugar Plums and Sherbet*, Totnes, 1999.

Masson, G., 'Food as a Fine Art in Seventeenth-Century Rome', *Apollo*, LXXXIII, 1966, pp. 338 - 41.

Musée National des Châteaux de Versailles et de Trianon, *Versailles et les Tables Royales en Europe, XVIIème- XIXème siècles*, Paris, 1994.

Paston-Williams, S., *The Art of Dining: A History of Cooking and Eating*, London, 1993.

Pietsch, U., *Schwanenservice: Meissener Porzellan für Heinrich Graf von Brühl*, Berlin, 2000.

Pinto, E. H., *Treen and other Wooden Bygones*, London, 1969.

Savill, R., 'A Sèvres treasure house at Waddesdon', *Apollo*, CXXXIX, 386, 1994, pp. 25-33.

Di Schino, June, *Tre Banchetti in onore di Christina di Svezia*, Rome, 2002.

Schwartz, S., 'A Feast for the Eyes: 18th-century Documents for the Creation of a Dessert Table', *International Ceramic Fair and Seminar* [Handbook], London, 2000, pp.28-35.

Stevenson, Sara and Thomson, Duncan, *John Michael Wright*, National Portrait Gallery, Edinburgh, 1982.

Werkener, P. 'J.P. Schor', *Alte und Moderne Kunst*, XXV, 1980, no. 169, pp.20-8.

Wheaton, B.K., *Savouring the Past: The French Kitchen and Table from 1300 to 1789*, London, 1983.

Plate 39 (see page 41)
Illustration of a pastry room/confectionery with a glass fronted case for storing sugar ornaments. Lithograph. From Urbain Dubois, *La Cuisine Artistique*, Paris, 1872. (Private Collection).

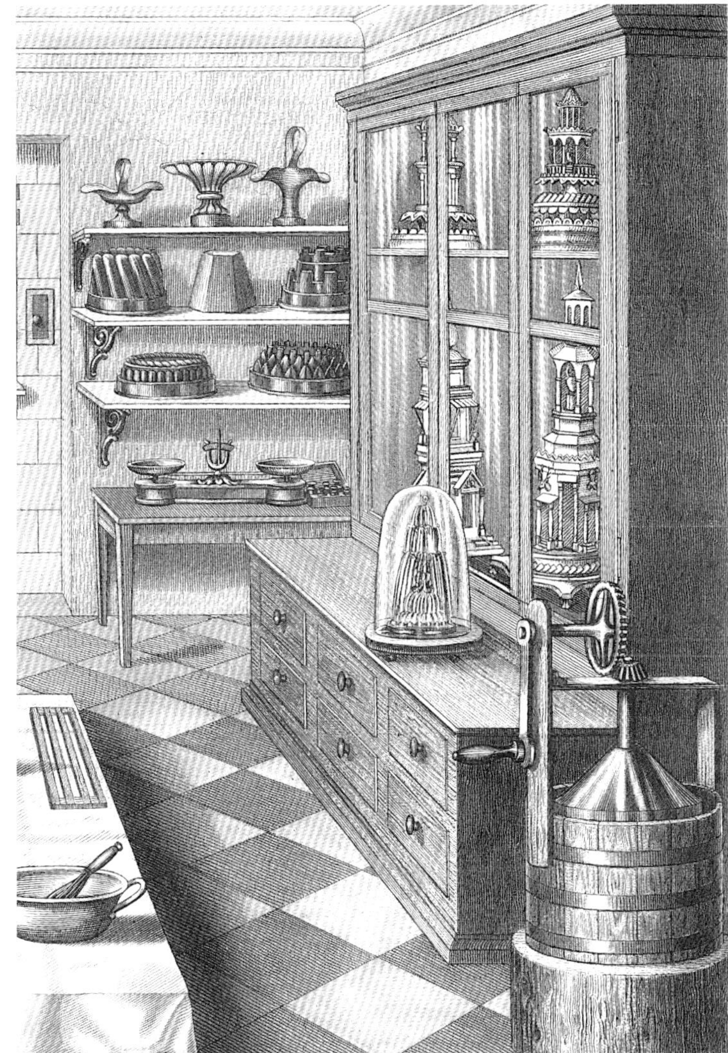

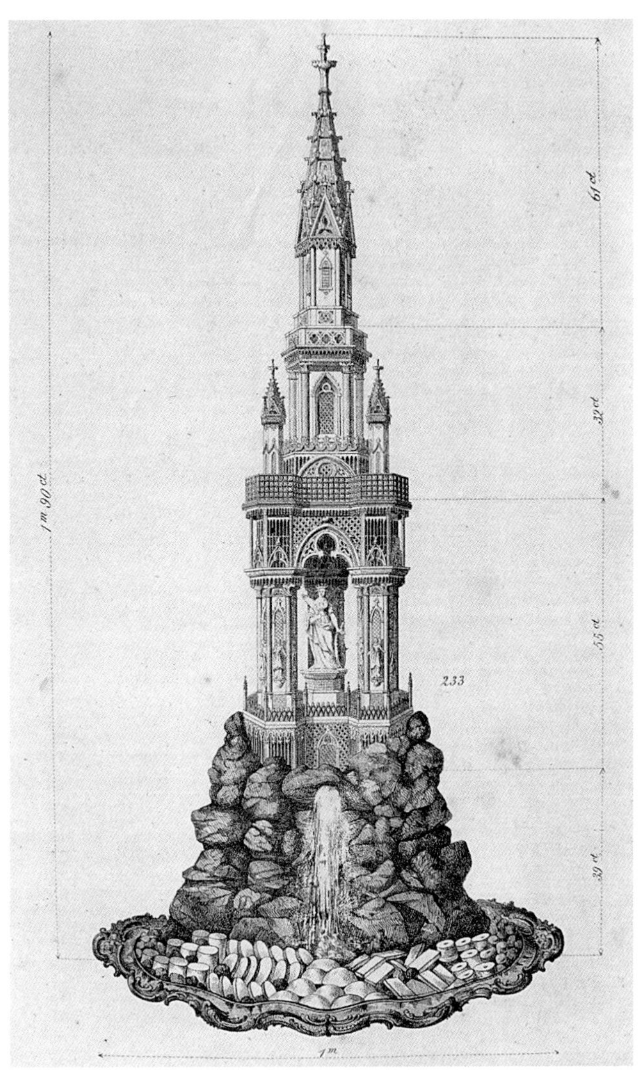

Plate 40 (see page 41)
Design for a gothic sugar centrepiece.
Illustration from Urbain Dubois and Emile Bernard, *La Cuisine Classique*, Paris, 1864.
(Private Collection).

References

1 Buonarroti il Giovane, Michelangelo, *Descrizione delle felicissime nozze della Christianissima Maesta di Madama Maria Medici, Regina di Francia e di Navarra*, Florence, 1600, p.16.

2 Ruscelli, Girolamo, *The Secretes of Maister Alexis Of Piemount*, Translated by Wyllyam Warde, London, 1558-69, pp.64-5.

3 Evans, Meryle, ' The Splendid Processions of Trade Guilds at Ottoman Festivals', in Walker, Harlan (ed.), *Food in the Arts*, Prospect Books, London, 1999.

4 Brears, Peter, *All the King's Cooks*, London, 1999, p.80.

5 Platt, Sir Hugh, *Delightes for Ladies*, London, 1600.

6 Jarrin, Gugliamo, *The Italian Confectioner*, London, 1820.

7 Le Grand d'Aussy, *La Vie Privée des François d'Autrefois*, ed. De Roquefort, II, p.317.

8 Anon. (1775), III, 244-6 (quoted in Brears, Peter, *All the King's Cooks*, London, 1999).

9 Probate Register Folio 13b/826r, Borthwick Institute of Historical Research, York.

10 Pinto, Edward, *Treen and other wooden bygones*, Bell and Hyman, London, 1976.

11 Geiger, Maureen Cassidy, 'Hof-Konditorei and Court Celebrations in 18th century Dresden', *The International Ceramics Fair, London* [Handbook], London, 2002, pp. 20-35.

12 Caird, J., *The Complete Confectioner and Family Cook*, Leith, 1809.

13 La Tang Fils, *Catalogue*, Paris, undated (late nineteenth century).

14 Laborde, Léon de, *Les Ducs de Bourgogne*, Paris,1851, Vol. 2, p. 338.

15 Day, Ivan, 'The Honours of the Table', in Brown, Peter, *British Cutlery*, Philip Wilson, London, 2001.

16 Fabyan, Robert, *The Chronicles of Fabyan*, London, 1516.

17 Cavendish, George, *The Life of Cardinal Wolsey*, London, 1893.

18 The novel idea of an edible chess set seems to have appealed to more recent diners. In the late nineteenth century, the New York company Eppelsheimer & Co. marketed a set of pewter moulds, which facilitated the production of a chess set made entirely of ice-cream.

19 Graminaeus, Theodor, *Beschreibung*...,Cologne, 1587.

20 Scappi, Bartolomeo, *Opera (Delle Arte del Cucinare)*,Venice, 1570.

21 Buonarroti il Giovane, Michelangelo, *op.cit.*, p.17.

22 Vasari, Giorgio, *Lives of the most Eminent Painters, Sculptors and Architects* [chapter devoted to Giovan Francesco Rustici], edition by Philip Lee Warner, London, Medici Society, 1912-15, pp.118-127.

23 Boucher, Bruce, *Baroque Sculpture*, Thames and Hudson, London, 1998, p.187.

24 Wright, John Michael, *Ragvaglio della solenne comparsa*..., Rome, 1687. An English version (not an exact translation) was published a year later in London as *An Account of his Excellence Roger, Earl of Castlemaine's Embassy*, London, 1688.

25 Ratta, Francesco, *Disegni del convito*, Bologna, 1693.

26 Corrado, Vicenzo, *Il credenziere di buon gusto*, Naples, 1778, pp.55-62.

27 Noever, Peter, MAK - *Austrian Museum of Applied Arts*, Munich, 1999, p.38.

28 Massiolot, François, *Nouvelle instruction pour les confitures*, Paris, 1692.

29 Eriksen, Svend, 'Rare Pieces of Vincennes and Sèvres Porcelain', *Apollo*, Jan. 1968, pp.38-39.

30 Heal, Ambrose, *London Tradesmen's Cards of the XVIII Century*, Batsford Ltd., London, 1925.

31 Shepherd, Rowena, *The Servery and Table Decker's Rooms at Osborne House* [unpublished report to English Heritage], 2000.

32 Kenny, Peter M., *Honoré Lannuier. Cabinet Maker from Paris*, New York, 1998, p.10.

33 Jarrin, *op.cit.*, p.198.

34 Jarrin, *op.cit.*, pp.197-8.

35 Nutt, Frederick, *The Complete Confectioner*, London, 1789.

36 Brown, Peter, 'Regency Ragoos and Royal Service', in Day, Ivan (ed.) *Eat Drink and be Merry*, Philip Wilson, London, 2000, p.81.

37 Jarrin, *op.cit.*, p.126.

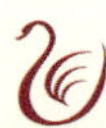